Careers in Science and Medicine

Susan Zannos

PO Box 619
Bear, Delaware 19701

Latinos at Work

Career Role Models for Young Adults

Careers in Community Service

Careers in Education

Careers in Entertainment

Careers in Law and Politics

Careers in the Music Industry

Careers in Publishing and Communications

Careers in Science and Medicine

Careers in Sports

Careers in Technology

Latino Entrepreneurs

Library of Congress Cataloging-In-Publication Data

Zannos, Susan.
　　Careers in science and medicine/Susan Zannos.
　　　　p. cm.—(Latinos at work)
　　Includes bibliographical references and index.
　　Summary: Explores career possibilities in science and medicine from a Latino perspective, focusing on the unique experiences of Hispanic Americans through interviews.
　　ISBN 1-58415-084-X
　　1. Science—Vocational guidance—United States—Juvenile literature. 2. Medicine—Vocational guidance—United States—Juvenile literature. 3. Hispanic Americans in science—Juvenile literature. 4. Hispanic Americans in medicine—Juvenile literature. [1. Hispanic Americans in science. 2. Hispanic Americans in medicine. 3. Science—Vocational guidance. 4. Medicine—Vocational guidance. 5. Vocational guidance.] I. Title. II. Series.
Q149.U5 Z36 2001
502'.3'73—dc21
　　　　　　　　　　　　　　　　　　　　　　　　　　　　2001038023

Careers in Science and Medicine

About the Author

Susan Zannos has been a lifelong educator, having taught at all levels, from preschool to college, in Mexico, Greece, Italy, Russia, and Lithuania, as well as in the United States. She has published a mystery *Trust the Liar* (Walker and Co.) and *Human Types: Essence and the Enneagram* was published by Samuel Weiser in 1997. She has written several books for children, including *Paula Abdul* and *Cesar Chavez* (Mitchell Lane). Susan lives in Oxnard, California.

Photo Credits

All photographs in this book were courtesy of the person being profiled.

Acknowledgments

The profiles of success depicted in Part Two were all written from the author's personal interviews. Interviews were conducted as follows:
Dr. Eloy Rodriguez: January 2001; Dr. Richard Tapia: January 23, 2001; Dr. Isabel Dominguez: January 25, 2001; Dr. Fidel Hernandez: February 5, 2001; Dr. Juana Acrivos: February 6, 2001; Dr. Teresa Ortega: February 6, 2001; Dr. Pedro Barbosa: February 7, 2001; Mr. Jose Alonso: February 9, 2001; Mr. Horacia Roa: January 30, 2001; Mr. Max Galinda: February 26, 2001.

Publishers Note

The careers depicted in this series are by no means all-inclusive. We have tried to show a representation of what is available by industry. Your career center at school or your local library can be of additional help identifying careers we might not have covered.

Contents

Part 1
Choosing a Career in Science or Medicine   **8**

Part 2
Profiles of Success   **35**

Part 3
Resources   **87**

Indexes   **92**

PART 1

Choosing a Career in Science or Medicine

· · · · · · · · · · · · · · · **TABLE OF CONTENTS** · · · · · · · · · · · · · · · ·

Careers in Science

Agriculturist	9	Dentist	19
Archaeologist	9	Laboratory Technician	20
Astronomer	10	Licensed Practical Nurse	20
Biologist	10	Medical Scientist	20
Chemist	11	Nurse	22
Engineer	11	Nursing Aide	23
Engineering Technician	12	Nutritionist	23
Forester	12	Optometrist	25
Geologist	13	Paramedic	26
Meteorologist	13	Pharmacist	26
Physicist	14	Physical Therapist	28
Science Technician	15	Physician	29

Careers in Healthcare

		Podiatrist	31
Acupuncturist	16	Psychiatrist	32
Chiropractor	17	Psychologist	32
Dental Hygienist	17	Veterinarian	33

Most careers in science and most careers in the health care professions require years of education, sometimes many years, beyond high school. The course work for both is based solidly on mathematics and science, so anyone planning to work in these areas will need an aptitude for and, it is hoped, enjoyment of these studies. At the level of graduate and postdoctoral research, there is no clear distinction between science and medicine. Many discoveries in the field of botany, for example, have medicinal applications, and zoologists studying animals learn much that can be applied to improve the health of humans.

Careers in Science

Latinos are underrepresented in science careers to an astonishing degree. This seems all the more peculiar since there is reason to believe that a strong aptitude for mathematics is generally characteristic of Hispanic populations. This was demonstrated dramatically by master teacher Jaime Escalante. He prepared so many of his Latino calculus students at Garfield High School in East Los Angeles to pass the difficult Advanced Placement Calculus tests in the 1980s and '90s that their accomplishments have made headlines all over the country.

Unfortunately, the teaching crisis in U.S. public schools severely affects the Latino population. Inner-city schools, the ones many Latino students attend, are the most seriously affected by the critical shortage of teachers who know enough math or science to teach classes at the secondary level. The few teachers who do have solid academic credentials in math and science are usually lured to better-paying jobs in wealthy suburban schools. This certainly doesn't mean that Latinos with an aptitude for science should give up! Far from it. It means that the problems faced can be seen as challenges and opportunities to excel. And there's nothing scientists seem to like better than meeting challenges and solving problems.

As the entomologist Dr. Pedro Barbosa observed (see Part 2), the courses become easier the further you go in academic work on the way to becoming a scientist. Don't make the mistake of thinking that if things are hard at first, it means they will just get harder later on. Mathematics classes may be difficult at first if you haven't been prepared well in junior high and high school, but once you do get the basics, the courses will become easier and easier for you. The one thing that all the Latino scientists interviewed for this book agree on is that once you find something that really interests you, it's important to hold on to it and not give up when you encounter obstacles. The greatest gift you can give yourself is to find something that really interests you to do for your life work. And the greatest gift you can give to the Latino community and to the young kids growing up is to be a role model so that they will see Latinos working in scientific careers and know that they can do it, too.

Selected Job Descriptions in Science

Agriculturalist

Agriculture and food scientists play an important part in maintaining the nation's food supply by ensuring production and safety of crops. A large percentage work for the federal, state, and local governments. *Plant scientists* work to increase both productivity and nutritional value of food crops. *Soil scientists* analyze the chemical makeup of the soil and make recommendations to farmers about land use. *Animal scientists* develop better and more efficient ways of producing and processing meat, poultry, eggs, and milk. *Food scientists* in private industry may work in test kitchens or laboratories. Soil scientists are likely to work outdoors. Animal scientists may work either in laboratories or in the field.

A bachelor's degree in agricultural science is enough for some jobs, but a master's degree or Ph.D. is usually required for research and teaching positions. Average growth is predicted for this field. Average federal salaries for plant and soil scientists are $54,000 and for animal scientists $70,000 per year. Median annual earnings for all agricultural and food scientists are $43,000.

Archaeologist

Archaeologists use scientific methods to excavate and study the remains of ancient civilizations in order to understand the prehistory of mankind. (Prehistory is the period before the development of written language.) Archaeology is also the study of cultures that did not develop written language, or whose languages have not been deciphered, and contributes to the understanding of many past civilizations. Excavations are done with great care and precision to preserve as well as possible the buildings and artifacts (human-made objects) that are covered with earth or with other more modern structures. By using carbon dating and other techniques, archaeologists are able to determine the time periods during which ancient cultures flourished. Archaeological expeditions, called digs, are usually funded by universities, private foundations, or the federal government, and sometimes by other nations. A Ph.D. is required for an archaeologist to receive such funding, but graduate students with bachelor's or master's degrees are also employed on digs. The growth potential for this field is above average because of laws requiring archaeological surveys as part of the environmental impact statements needed by land developers. The median annual salary for archaeologists is $45,000.

Astronomer

The objective of an astronomer is to understand the nature of the universe. It takes a special person to try this, one who likes to challenge and be challenged. It is useful to take as much math as possible in high school, and chemistry and physics courses as well, to have a solid foundation in this field. The best preparation for graduate work in astronomy is either an astronomy major with a minor in physics or a physics major with some astronomy course work. Computer science is also necessary for this field. Most astronomy positions require a Ph.D., which can take five or six years of graduate work to obtain.

About 60 percent of jobs in astronomy are in academia, 30 percent are in government and national observatories, 5 percent are in museums and public information services, and 5 percent are in business and private industry. The average salary for astronomers is $77,000 per year.

Biologist

Biological scientists study living organisms and their relationship to the environment. Nearly all these scientists work in research and development, which continues to provide solutions to human health problems and to preserve and repair the natural environment. *Aquatic biologists* study plants and animals living in water. Of these, *marine biologists* study saltwater organisms and *limnologists* study freshwater organisms. *Ecologists* study the relationship among organisms and between organisms and their environment. *Entomologists* specialize in the study of insects, and *microbiologists* investigate the growth and characteristics of microscopic organisms such as bacteria, algae, and fungi. *Zoologists* study the origin, behavior, and life processes of animals.

A Ph.D. is usually required for biological research and teaching positions. Although the growth rate in this field is faster than average, there is a lot of competition for research positions. The federal government funds much of the basic research and development. Colleges, universities, and private industry also employ biological scientists. The median annual earnings of biological scientists are about $47,000, with the lowest 10 percent earning less than $28,000 and the highest 10 percent earning more than $86,000.

Chemist

Everything in our environment, whether natural or human-made, is composed of chemicals. Chemists do research that provides new knowledge about chemicals. This knowledge is applied to the development of synthetic fibers, paints, drugs, cosmetics, electronic components, and thousands of other products. Chemists often specialize. For example, *analytical chemists* examine and identify the elements that make up a substance.

Organic chemists study the chemistry of the carbon compounds that make up all living things. *Inorganic chemists* study compounds made up of elements other than carbon, such as those used in electronics. *Physical chemists* study the physical characteristics of atoms and molecules. *Biochemists* work in both biology and chemistry.

Nearly half of all chemists are employed by manufacturing firms. Other employers are federal agencies, state and local governments, and colleges and universities. The growth rate of this field is average. A bachelor's degree in chemistry is the minimum requirement for entry-level jobs, and many research positions require a Ph.D. Median annual salary of chemists with a bachelor's degree is $50,000 per year; with a master's $61,000; and with a Ph.D. $76,000.

Engineer

Engineers apply the theories and principles of science and mathematics to find solutions to practical problems. Their work connects scientific discoveries and the design of new products, machines to produce the products, factories in which to produce them, and systems to ensure the quality of the products. Most engineers specialize: There are more than 25 major engineering specialties, each with many subdivisions. Engineers in each branch have basic knowledge and training that can be applied in many fields. *Electrical engineers,* for example, work in medical, computer, missile guidance, and power distribution engineering. *Aerospace engineers* develop technologies for use in aviation, defense systems, and space exploration. *Chemical engineers* are employed in industries producing pharmaceuticals, chemical cleaning agents, and petroleum products. *Civil engineers* plan and build highways, bridges, dams, and water treatment systems. *Industrial engineers* study the efficient use of personnel, materials, and machines in factories, shops, stores, and offices. *Mechanical engineers* design, develop, test, and manufacture industrial machinery. There are over 1.5 million engineering jobs, almost half of which are in manufacturing industries.

A bachelor's degree is required for entry-level engineering jobs; most degrees are granted in electrical, mechanical, or civil engineering. Graduate training is necessary for engineering faculty positions. Employment opportunities for engineers are good. There is a great variation in pay scales for engineers, depending on the industry they are in and the amount of experience they have; the median annual salary of engineers is $45,000.

Engineering Technician

The work of technicians is more limited in scope and more practically oriented than that of engineers. Most engineering technicians specialize in a particular area, just as engineers do. Nearly half of them work in the electronics field. Although there may be a few jobs not requiring formal training, most employers prefer to hire someone with at least an associate's degree in engineering technology. Training is available at technical institutions, community colleges, and vocational schools. This employment field has average growth potential. The median annual salary of engineering technicians is $33,000.

Forester

Foresters and conservation scientists manage, develop, and help protect forests and rangelands that serve as recreation areas and habitats for wildlife as well as producing wood products and livestock forage. Over 60 percent of these scientists work for federal, state, or local governments. Some work outdoors in all types of weather, sometimes in isolated areas. They may need to walk long distances through densely wooded land or spend long hours fighting fires. They may provide emergency help after such natural disasters as forest fires, floods, mud slides, or tropical storms. A bachelor's degree in forestry is the minimum requirement for professional careers in forestry. Foresters who want to do specialized research would need an advanced degree. The growth rate in this field is average. The median annual salary of conservation scientists and foresters is $43,000. Starting salaries in state and local government positions are usually lower than those in the federal government or private industry.

Geologist

Geologists and geophysicists study the physical characteristics and history of the earth. They frequently work at remote field sites. They identify and examine rocks, conduct geological surveys, construct maps, and use instruments to measure gravity and magnetic fields. They collect and analyze information collected by seismic prospecting, which involves bouncing sound waves off buried layers of rock. *Geoscientists* play an important part in studying, preserving, and cleaning up the environment. *Petroleum geologists* search for oil; *mineralogists* analyze and classify mineral deposits and precious stones. *Geological oceanographers* study and map the ocean floor using remote sensing devices from surface ships. *Seismologists* study earthquakes and try to find ways to predict them.

A bachelor's degree is sufficient for some entry-level jobs, but there are more job opportunities for candidates with master's degrees. Beginning annual salaries for geologists with a bachelor's degree are around $35,000, with a master's degree around $45,000. A Ph.D. is required for research positions in universities or federal agencies. The growth rate for this career is average. The median annual salary of geologists is $54,000. The petroleum and mining industries sometimes pay over $100,000 per year for geologists with advanced degrees.

Meteorologist

Meteorology is the study of the air that surrounds the earth. Meteorologists study the atmosphere's physical characteristics, motions, and processes and the way it affects the rest of the environment. The most familiar use of meteorology is in weather forecasting, but it is also used for pollution control, predicting safety of air and sea transportation, and the study of global warming or ozone-layer loss. The largest group of specialists are *operational meteorologists*, the "weathermen" who study air pressure, temperature, humidity, wind velocity, and other factors to make long- and short-term weather predictions. *Physical meteorologists* study the atmosphere's chemical and physical properties; transmission of light, sound, and radio waves; and transfer of energy. *Climatologists* analyze past records of wind, rainfall, and temperature in specific regions.

Most meteorologists are employed by the federal government. The growth rate in this field will decline slightly. Average starting salaries vary according to education: with a bachelor's degree, $20,000; a master's degree, $25,000; and a doctorate, $36,000 per year. Median annual earnings of meteorologists are $55,000.

Physicist

Physicists explore and identify basic principles governing the structure and behavior of matter, the generation and transfer of energy, and the interaction of matter and energy. Based on observation and analysis, they attempt to discover and explain laws governing the forces of nature, such as gravity, electromagnetism, and nuclear interactions. Most physicists work in research and development. For instance, basic research in solid-state physics led to the development of transistors and then to the integrated circuits used in computers.

Physicists are employed by federal agencies such as the Department of Defense and the National Aeronautics and Space Administration (NASA), as well as by universities and private manufacturing companies. A Ph.D. is usually required for research in physics, although some colleges offer master's programs that prepare students for research and development in private industry, or for teaching at the high school or junior college level. Growth rate in this field is slower than average. Median annual earnings for physicists are $74,000, with the lowest 10 percent earning less than $42,000 and the highest 10 percent more than $114,000.

Science Technician

The jobs of science technicians are more practically oriented than the jobs of scientists. Technicians set up, operate, and maintain laboratory instruments, monitor experiments, calculate and record results, and keep detailed accounts of all their activities. Those who work in production ensure quality by testing products. Technicians specialize just as scientists do. Most work indoors, usually in laboratories, and have regular hours; *production technicians* frequently work in eight-hour shifts around the clock. Most employers prefer applicants who have at least two years of specialized training or an associate's degree in applied science, although some require a bachelor's degree. Many technical and community colleges offer two-year degrees in specific technologies. Median hourly earnings for science technicians are about $15. Starting positions for technicians in the federal government are paid $16,500 per year.

Medicine

There is a very great and rapidly growing need for Latinos in the health care professions. As the Spanish-speaking population in the United States continues to grow, it becomes more and more crucial to have doctors, nurses, paramedics, pharmacists, and other health practitioners who are bilingual and can communicate with their patients in their primary language. It is also essential that caregivers understand and share the culture of their patients. Because the need is so great, qualified candidates of Hispanic background can obtain financial assistance in the form of scholarships, grants, student loans, and other aids that will enable them to complete their education.

Most of the jobs in health care require some education beyond a high school or equivalency diploma, and some require a great deal more education. Doctors, for example, frequently are required to study for 12 or more years after high school, although during the final years of internship and residency they are paid for their services. There is, however, a direct correlation between the time spent in higher education and the amount of money to be earned in a given career field. The time and effort spent in college or vocational school might seem difficult to invest, but they are rewarded with a more comfortable lifestyle for the worker and his or her family for a lifetime.

In addition to economic benefits, jobs in health care offer the satisfaction of knowing one is helping others. Making a positive contribution to the health and well-being of the community and easing the suffering of those who are struggling with diseases or injuries can increase the emotional and spiritual health of the practitioner. These jobs can, of course, also be very stressful, so it is important to be sure that one has the character and aptitudes necessary for successful practice.

For anyone considering a career in the medical field, a lot of mathematics and science courses are required, so your success in and attitude toward such classes as algebra and calculus, biology and chemistry is an important indicator of your success and contentment in this field. Perhaps more important is the ability to work effectively with people. In health care, communication is essential. The ability to make oneself clearly understood and the ability to listen carefully and

sensitively to what others say are vital. One must inspire confidence and trust in the patients and in other members of the health care team. For this reason many medical schools prefer candidates with English or speech majors over those with science majors.

Getting practical experience that will let you know whether a particular career is right for you is as important as academic ability. Fortunately there are many opportunities to get such experience in the health care field. Volunteers are always welcome in hospitals, nursing homes, and rehabilitation centers. By spending time doing some of the simpler caregiving tasks, such as feeding patients who are unable to feed themselves, seeing that they have fresh water, or running errands for them, the volunteer will have the opportunity to experience and observe the work of health care practitioners.

Part-time jobs as nurses' aides and orderlies are almost always available in hospitals and nursing homes or custodial care facilities. These positions are available in the evenings and on weekends when the regular staff wants time off, so it is possible to experience the world of health care work and be paid for it. Since there is a large investment of time and money in advanced education, it is important to be sure you have the capabilities required before committing yourself. If you faint at the sight of blood, you probably should consider some other career—maybe in science rather than medicine.

Selected Job Descriptions in Health Care

● ●

Acupuncturist

Acupuncture, an ancient Chinese healing art, has been practiced for thousands of years and is rapidly gaining acceptance in the United States. Acupuncturists treat symptoms and disorders by inserting very thin needles in specific points on the body to stimulate the flow of energy. This energy, or *chi,* flows along specific pathways, called meridians, and disease results when the *chi* is blocked or unbalanced. After placing the needles the acupuncturist may apply heat or a low electric current to them.

There are more than 50 schools of acupuncture in the United States. Some offer only certificate or bachelor's degree programs; others offer master's degree programs. Most training programs provide education in all aspects of traditional Chinese medicine. Many medical doctors take acupuncture as part of their medical training. Licensing and certification vary widely from state to state. Most acupuncturists operate their own private practices or form partnerships with other alternative health practitioners. The average salary of acupuncturists who have worked ten years or more is $30,000 per year, but this should increase along with greater public acceptance of this therapy.

Chiropractor

Chiropractic medicine is a health field that treats muscular, nervous, and skeletal systems, concentrating especially on the spine. The basic theory behind this practice is that many diseases are caused by incorrect spinal alignment and can be treated by manipulating the spine. Chiropractic emphasizes a holistic view that stresses overall well-being with natural, nondrug, and nonsurgical health treatment. Some chiropractors specialize in sports injuries, some in interpreting X rays, some in treating children. The projected growth rate for

Working as a Bilingual Dentist

Fillmore, California, is a small agricultural community nestled among rolling hills of orange and lemon groves in Ventura County. The population is 60 percent Spanish-speaking, with many recent immigrants who speak very little English. Fortunately these people have a bilingual dentist, Dr. Guillermo Sanchez, to tend to their dental needs.

Guillermo was born in Colombia in 1967 and came to California when he was three years old. His father was already a practicing dentist in Colombia, but he had to retake much of his training to meet the licensing requirements in the United States. He did this at UCLA, then began a successful dental practice. While Guillermo was growing up he sometimes went with his dad to the office, but he had no intention of becoming a dentist—in fact, he said his mind was closed to the possibility.

After graduating in 1985 from LaSalle High School, a private Catholic school in Pasadena, he enrolled at the University of California at Irvine, where he enjoyed his science classes. Because he liked science, Guillermo thought he might want to be a doctor, so he talked to some physicians to find out what their jobs were like. When they told him what long hours they worked, how they had to be on call much of the time, and the amount of training and internship that would be required even after medical school, Guillermo decided that medicine was not for him.

Meanwhile he needed a part-time job to help with his college expenses. He answered several ads, but the positions were always filled before he got there. Finally he applied for one at the university health clinic, got the job—and found out it was in the dental clinic. Furthermore, he discovered he liked the work. He also learned that he could begin practicing after four years of dental school and would not need to specialize the way 80 percent of doctors do. He started to rethink his resistance to becoming a dentist. When he graduated from UC Irvine, he went to dental school at Loma Linda University in San Bernardino, graduating in 1993.

Guillermo's father had problems with his practice in Glendale when the lease on his office space was not renewed. The elder Dr. Sanchez was told about Fillmore, where there was a large Spanish-speaking population and no Latino dentist, so he decided to practice there part-time, commuting from their home in Arcadia. Guillermo joined his father in this practice, which grew larger and larger until it was full-time for both of them. As his father aged, the younger Dr. Sanchez took over more and more of the work until his father retired.

While continuing his dental practice in Fillmore, Dr. Guillermo Sanchez is planning to open a second office soon, in nearby Moorpark, where he lives. When asked what he likes least about his job, he said the managerial part—dealing with employees, insurance companies, and red tape in general. What he likes best is the freedom to set his own schedule—to come in when he wants and schedule vacations when he wants. He also enjoys the interaction with his patients, helping people out and talking to them in their native language.

this career is above average. The licensing of chiropractors is regulated by the states: All require completion of a four-year chiropractic college course leading to the Doctor of Chiropractic degree. (Most colleges of chiropractic require a bachelor's degree for admission.)

In chiropractics, as in other types of independent practice, earnings are relatively low in the beginning and increase as the practice grows. Earnings are influenced by the characteristics and qualifications of the practitioner, number of years in practice, and geographical location. The average income of all chiropractors is about $85,000, while practitioners in the top 10 percent earn more than $170,000 per year.

Dental Hygienist

Dental hygienists clean teeth, take and develop X rays, and provide other preventive dental care. Flexible scheduling is a feature of this job since full-time, part-time, evening, and weekend work is widely available. Many dentists hire hygienists to work only two or three days a week, so hygienists may work in more than one location. To qualify to be licensed by the state in which they practice, dental hygienists must graduate from an accredited dental hygiene school and pass both a written and clinical examination. Most programs offer an associate's degree, which means the training can be completed in two years. This is one of the 30 fastest growing occupations, since improvements in dentistry mean greater retention of natural teeth. The median earnings of dental hygienists are $23 per hour. The lowest 10 percent earned less than $13 and the highest 10 percent more than $39 per hour.

Dentist

Dentists diagnose and treat diseases of the teeth and mouth, take and examine mouth X rays, fill cavities, straighten and repair teeth, and treat gum disease. All states require dentists to be licensed, which means they must graduate from a school accredited by the American Dental Association and pass written and practical examinations. Candidates must have at least two years of college before being admitted to dental school, and most dental students have at least a bachelor's degree with emphasis on course work in the sciences. Most dentists are general practitioners,

although some are specialists such as *orthodontists*, who straighten teeth, or *oral surgeons,* who operate on the mouth. Other specialties are *pediatric dentistry*, for treating children; *periodontics*, for treating gum disease; and *prosthodontics*, for making and fitting false teeth.

The growth rate for the field of dentistry is lower than average. In dentistry, specialists usually earn more than general practitioners. The average income for general practitioners is $109,000 per year, while specialists average $175,000 per year.

Laboratory Technician

Clinical laboratory testing plays an important role in the detection, diagnosis, and treatment of disease. Lab technicians perform many of these tests. They examine and analyze body fluids, tissues, and cells; they match blood types for transfusions and test for drug levels in the blood. *Histology technicians* cut and stain tissue specimens for microscopic examination, and *phlebotomists* collect blood samples.

Medical and clinical laboratory technicians generally have either an associate's degree from a community or junior college or a certificate from a hospital or vocational school. A few learn their skills on the job. The growth rate of this field is about average. The median annual earnings of laboratory technicians are about $26,000.

Licensed Practical Nurse

Licensed practical nurses (LPNs), or licensed vocational nurses, as they are called in Texas and California, are frequently trained in vocational or technical schools in programs lasting about one year. They provide basic bedside care for patients; monitor vital signs such as temperature, blood pressure, pulse, and respiration; collect samples for testing; and feed and bathe patients. About one-third of LPNs work in hospitals, and another third in nursing homes. Others may be employed by temporary help agencies, home health care services, or in doctors' offices. Employment in this field will have average growth. Median annual earnings are $27,000 per year.

Medical Scientist

Medical scientists do basic research into normal biological systems to understand the causes of disease and other health problems and to discover treatments. They try to identify changes in a cell, a chromosome, or even in a gene that may signal the development of medical problems, such as different types of cancer. A Ph.D. is usually necessary for medical scientists who do independent research, while a master's degree may be sufficient for jobs in applied research or product development. A bachelor's degree is adequate for some non-research jobs such as testing and inspection or technical sales. A bachelor's degree may also qualify a medical laboratory technician for this job. The growth rate for this career field is greater than average. Beginning salaries for medical scientists with a bachelor's degree are about $30,000 per year; with a master's, $35,000; and with a Ph.D., $46,000.

Nurse

Registered nurses (RNs) form the largest health care occupation, with over 2 million jobs. Registered nurse is in the top 10 occupations predicted to have the largest number of new jobs. Earnings are above average, particularly for nurses who specialize and have additional training. *Hospital nurses* are the largest group of nurses. They provide bedside care for patients, carry out medical regimens, and supervise licensed practical nurses and aides.

Meet Horacio Roa, Alternative Medical Practitioner

The medical techniques practiced by most physicians in the United States are not the only ones in the world. Practitioners in alternative medicine think that Western medicine may not always have the best therapies for some people and in some situations. These health care providers learn, and practice, other methods of healing. Horacio Roa is one of these—a practitioner of holistic medicine, which is treatment of the whole person, not just the person's symptoms or illnesses.

Horacio was born in Buenos Aires, Argentina, in 1961 to parents who had moved there from Paraguay. His grandfather on his mother's side was a healer among the Guarni Indians of Paraguay. "The healing art is part of our culture," Horacio says. He remembers that people would come to his grandfather's house to ask for help in healing different things. "He wasn't a professional because he didn't want to become a professional. He did it because he liked to help people."

Horacio's interest in healing started because he needed to heal himself. He was often sick as a child. From the time he was four years old he had a persistent cough that was treated with antibiotics and codeine, standard treatment in Western medicine. By the time he was 15 years old he was overweight and had asthma, headaches, and psychological and emotional difficulties. He was a sick teenager. He began experimenting with a vegetarian diet, and then a macrobiotic diet. They produced good results, so he studied nutrition and became a dietary technician in Argentina.

He also began studying yoga when he was 15, and then he taught yoga classes. Yoga is a system of stretching, relaxation, and breathing exercises that originated in India. Later he also studied Chinese medicine and practiced shiatsu, which is based on the Chinese techniques of acupuncture but does not use needles. Like acupuncture, shiatsu is designed to help the flow of energy, or *chi,* in the body. But instead of stimulation with needles at the points where the energy is blocked, shiatsu practitioners use massage and acupressure.

In 1987 Horacio went to Madrid, Spain, where he studied herbology, the use of herbs for healing. He observes that herbs cannot do the harm that manufactured drugs do. "Chemicals come from herbs," Horacio says, "but the process changes their molecular structure and they can have secondary effects. Herbs are more innocent. They are the oldest medicines in our civilization."

Horacio also studied homeopathy in Spain. Homeopaths look at illness differently than traditional Western doctors do. They feel that illnesses are symptoms of a larger problem and believe that treating the illness is not always the best approach. They are more likely to use medicines that have the same effects as the illness in an attempt to stimulate the body's natural healing powers. In his studies of holistic medicine, Horacio looked for people who were healers, "not people who were conventional, not official doctors," he says. "First I asked them to treat me. Then I asked them to teach me."

Horacio Roa came to the United States in 1994 and now works in a clinic in a rural area near the town of Dobbins in the Sierra foothills of northern California. He is licensed as a massage therapist with the Association of Body Workers and is in practice with his wife, Laura, a nurse-practitioner who is also experienced in the principles and practices of holistic medicine.

They are usually assigned to one area such as surgery, maternity, pediatrics, emergency room, or intensive care, although some nurses may rotate among departments.

Office nurses care for outpatients in physicians' offices, clinics, and emergency medical centers. They assist with examinations, administer medications, assist with minor surgery, and maintain records. *Public health nurses* work in government and private agencies and clinics, in schools, and in other community settings. They instruct individuals and groups in health education, disease prevention, and child care; they arrange for immunizations and health screening tests. At the highest level of this profession, *nurse-practitioners* provide basic primary health care, diagnosing and treating common acute illnesses and injuries.

In all states, students must graduate from a nursing program and pass a national licensing examination. There are two types of nursing degrees, a two-year associate's degree in nursing and a four-year bachelor of science degree in nursing. Many nurses get an A.D.N. (associate's degree in nursing) and then work while continuing their education for a B.S.N. (bachelor of science in nursing), often with their employers reimbursing them for their tuition. The median annual earnings of registered nurses are $41,000, with the lowest 10 percent making less than $30,000 and the highest 10 percent making more than $70,000.

Nursing Aide

Nursing and psychiatric aides help care for physically or mentally ill, injured, or disabled patients confined to hospitals, nursing or residential care facilities, or mental health settings. They serve meals, help feed and bathe patients and make them comfortable, and are often the principle caregivers in nursing homes. *Psychiatric aides,* also called *mental health technicians,* may socialize with mentally ill patients and lead them in educational and recreational activities (see Spotlight Story page 32.) In many instances neither a high school diploma nor previous experience is necessary for employment as aides (although many positions may require on-the-job training); therefore these occupations can provide an entry into the world of health care employment. Since patients must be cared for 24 hours each day, jobs are available for any shift, which means these jobs are available to students who must work to finance their educations and to others who need the flexibility of night and weekend hours. Employment in this field will grow faster than average because of the rapidly growing elderly population. Median earnings of aides, orderlies, and attendants are $8 per hour; median earnings of psychiatric aides are $11 per hour.

Nutritionist

Dietitians and nutritionists plan food and nutrition programs and supervise the preparation and serving of meals. They help prevent and treat illnesses by promoting healthy eating habits. *Clinical dietitians* provide nutritional services for patients in institutions such as hospitals and nursing homes.

Community dietitians counsel groups and individuals, working in places such as public health clinics. *Management dietitians* oversee large-scale meal planning and preparation in company cafeterias, prisons, and schools. Increased interest in nutrition has led to opportunities in food manufacturing, advertising, and marketing as well. Dietitians and nutritionists need at least a bachelor's degree and must pass a certification exam after completing academic work. Median annual earnings are $35,000.

Optometrist

Over half the people in the United States wear glasses or contact lenses. Optometrists, or doctors of optometry, provide most primary vision care. They examine people's eyes to diagnose vision problems and eye diseases, but they should not be confused with ophthalmologists, physicians who perform eye surgery and treat eye diseases. All states require optometrists to be licensed. They must graduate from an accredited optometry school and pass written and clinical state board examinations. Licenses must be renewed every few years, which requires continuing education credits. Growth potential in this field is average.

Optometrists may be employed either by health care organizations or by franchised optical stores, or they may go into private practice. New optometry graduates in their first year of practice earn an average of $55,000, while the median net income for all optometrists is $92,000 per year.

Paramedic

People's lives often depend on the quick action and competent care of paramedics and emergency medical technicians (EMTs; see Spotlight Story p. 29.) Women giving birth and victims of automobile accidents, heart attacks, drownings, gunshot or knife wounds, and drug overdoses all require immediate medical attention. Depending on the nature of the emergency, paramedics and EMTs are dispatched to the scene by a 911 or other emergency operator and often work with police and firemen. When they arrive on the scene, they determine the patient's condition. Following strict procedures, they give appropriate emergency care and transport the patient. They usually work as partners, with one driving the emergency vehicle while the other cares for the patient. Some who work for trauma centers may be part of a helicopter flight crew.

Irregular hours and life-or-death emergency situations make this a stressful occupation. Paramedics and EMTs are employed by private ambulance services, hospitals, and fire departments. This field is projected to grow rapidly. Training has progressive levels: *EMT Basic, EMT Intermediate,* and *EMT Paramedic,* each level requiring more course work and field experience. Earnings depend on geographical location and type of employment setting as well as on amount of training. The median salary for paramedics is $21,000 per year.

Pharmacist

The traditional work of pharmacists, the mixing and preparation of medicines, has become a very small part of their practice since most medicines are now produced by pharmaceutical companies in standard dosages. About 60 percent of pharmacists work in retail pharmacies, some as self-employed owners and some as employees of drugstore chains. They counsel patients, answer questions about prescriptions and over-the-counter drugs, and make recommendations. Pharmacists in hospitals and clinics dispense medications and advise the medical staff on the effects of different drugs. A license to practice pharmacy is required in all states. To obtain a license one must graduate from an accredited college of pharmacy, pass a state examination, and serve an internship under a licensed pharmacist. Most colleges of pharmacy require one or two years of college work before an applicant can be accepted to their program. Employment is expected to grow slower than the average due to automation of drug dispensing and greater use of technicians. The median annual income of pharmacists is $67,000.

Physical Therapist

Physical therapists provide services that help restore functions, improve mobility, relieve pain, and promote overall fitness and health. Treatment often includes exercise and may also use electrical stimulation, heat pads, and ultrasound. Physical therapists often consult and practice with other professionals such as physicians, nurses, occupational therapists, and social workers. All states require passing a licensing exam after graduating from an accredited physical therapist educational program. These programs are required to offer degrees at the master's level and above. Employment

Working as a Family Doctor

Dr. Guadalupe Zamora's day begins early. She arrives at the hospital at 6:30 A.M. to make her rounds, which means checking on her patients to see how they're progressing, what kind of night they've had, and whether they are having any problems she needs to tend to. She goes to her office at 8:30 or 9:00 A.M., and usually works through lunch because she has so many patients to see. After the working day at the office ends at 5:00 P.M., when her staff goes home, Dr. Zamora usually has one or two hospital admissions to make, so she usually finishes her day there. Most days she gets home around 7:00 or 7:30 P.M.

When she was in medical school, Guadalupe was undecided as to whether she wanted to be a family practitioner or a pediatrician. "I've always enjoyed talking to the Hispanic *abuelitas* (grandmothers). They always tell you great stories," she says. "During Christmas we get so much food—*tamalitos* here, other things there—that's what really made me decide to go into family practice."

Dr. Zamora thinks that her ability to speak Spanish has been a great benefit in her career. "As you well know," she says, "we have a growing Hispanic population in the country, and many patients, although they speak some English, prefer to speak Spanish. So that's my special talent. I listen and I speak the language." She feels there are three As to a successful medical practice: being available, being affable (friendly), and being affordable. When her patients can't pay, she tells them not to worry about it.

When asked what she likes best about her job, Dr. Zamora says that it's being able to make people better, especially children. "When they're sick, they don't feel good and they want to get better right away. I always try to be available to them. That's the most exciting thing to me."

is expected to grow faster than average. The median annual income of physical therapists is $57,000.

Physician

Physicians perform medical examinations, diagnose illnesses, and treat people who are suffering from injury or disease. They also advise patients on good health practices. There are two types of physicians: the M.D., doctor of medicine; and the D.O., doctor of osteopathy. Physicians may be general practitioners or they may specialize. About one-third are primary care physicians or in family practice and tend to see the same patients on a regular basis (see Spotlight Story p. 27). Most M.D.s are specialists. *Anesthesiologists* work with surgeons in operating rooms, sedating patients and monitoring their vital signs during surgery or childbirth. *Dermatologists* specialize in diseases of the skin; *gastroenterologists,* diseases of the digestive system; *ophthalmologists,* diseases of the eyes. *Obstetrician/ gynecologists* specialize in women's reproductive health, including prenatal care and delivering babies, and *pediatricians* care for the infant after it is delivered and throughout childhood. Many physicians specialize in the treatment of specific diseases, as *oncologists* treat cancer patients and *cardiologists* treat patients with heart disease. *Surgeons* operate on patients to remove diseased tissues, correct abnormal conditions, or repair damage done in accidents; *plastic surgeons* frequently do cosmetic surgery to change people's appearance. These are only a few examples of the many, many medical specialties.

Physicians are much more likely now to work as salaried employees of group medical practices, clinics, or health care networks than in the past. Their formal education and training are among the longest of any occupation. The training required is usually four years of undergraduate college work leading to a bachelor's degree, four years of medical school, and three to eight years of internship and residency (which is paid on-the-job training), depending on the specialty. The growth rate for this career is faster than average. Physicians have among the highest average annual earnings of any occupation, although earnings vary according to specialty, years in practice, geographic location, hours worked, and the physician's skill, personality, and professional reputation. Beginning

Meet Max Galindo, Paramedic

Max Galindo is a paramedic working out of one of the five emergency stations manned by the Gold Coast Ambulance Service in Oxnard, California. He works a 24-hour shift every other day—7:00 in the morning until 7:00 the next morning. Every month the paramedics get six consecutive days off to get rested up. This means they work only 10 to 12 days a month, but the total number of hours worked still adds up to an average of about 70 hours a week.

When they arrive at the station to begin their shift, the paramedics, who work in pairs, check out their ambulance with all their equipment. Then they have a briefing that informs them of what went on during the previous 24 hours and of current conditions in the area and any changes of routine or paperwork that they need to be aware of. Max says that the average number of calls they receive on a given 24-hour shift is about seven or eight. "If there are as many as twelve, it's terrible—you don't eat, you don't sleep. Fifteen is a nightmare."

Common calls are from people with difficulty breathing, chest pains, diabetic problems, and of course from those in auto accidents. "We do see some pretty gory things, but usually when it's that bad the patient is dead and we don't have to do anything. It's the calls where the patient is between life and death where we do have to function. The only ones that affect me a lot are the children. Those are the only real difficult calls. . . . It hurts me to see kids who are sick or injured."

Because Max Galindo is bilingual, he is able to communicate with his patients in both English and Spanish. Since over half the population in the area in which he works is Spanish-speaking, this ability is important.

He describes the paramedic course as "like medical school in one year's time. They cram that information into a matter of months. It's very, very intense, from eight in the morning to five at night, and then a lot of studying."

The main drawback to his job, Max feels, is low pay—$9 per hour to start. But he likes having the time off because it allows him to spend time with his two children, who are six and four years old.

salaries for resident physicians, who are doctors still in training, are around $35,000 per year. General practitioners have median earnings of $130,000 per year, while in some specialties the median earnings are over $250,000 per year.

Podiatrist

Also known as doctors of podiatric medicine (DPMs), podiatrists diagnose and treat disorders and diseases of the foot and lower leg. The human foot is a complex structure containing 26 bones plus muscles, nerves, ligaments, and blood vessels. The 52 bones of the feet make up one-quarter of the bones in the body. Podiatrists treat corns, calluses, ingrown toenails, bunions, and other deformities. Other conditions treated by podiatrists include ankle and foot injuries and foot complaints associated with diseases such as diabetes. Some practitioners specialize in surgery, orthopedics, or public health. Podiatrists may choose subspecialty areas such as sports medicine, pediatrics, dermatology, geriatrics, or diabetic foot care.

The growth rate for the field is slower than average. All states require a license for the practice of podiatric medicine. Generally the applicant must be a graduate of an accredited college of podiatric medicine in addition to having undergraduate degrees, and he or she must pass written and oral examinations. Most states also require a residency program. Podiatrists usually have their own practice and therefore need to have business skills. Their income rises significantly as their practice grows. Those practicing less than 2 years earn an average of $60,000; those practicing 16 to 30 years earn an average of $145,000 per year.

Psychiatrist

Psychiatrists treat patients whose emotional problems make it hard for them to function in society. These problems might stem from common ailments such as anxiety, depression, eating disorders, or addiction to drugs and alcohol, or from less common disorders such as schizophrenia. Psychiatrists may use psychoanalysis, which is a method of helping the patient bring unconscious fears and conflicts into the conscious mind through talking; they frequently use medications to help the patient control undesirable behaviors. After high school, it takes between 12 and 14 years of schooling and training to become a psychiatrist: four years of undergraduate school, four years of medical school, and four years of psychiatric residency. Child psychiatrists, for instance, must have three years of general residency and two years in child psychiatry. The growth rate in this field is potentially large. The average income for all psychiatrists is $135,000 per year, but there is a very large range of incomes depending on geographical location and specialty.

Psychologist

Unlike psychiatrists, psychologists are not medical doctors, although they also deal with mental health and are specialists in human behavior. The field of psychology is divided into many specialties. *Clinical psychology* is the largest area of specialization. These therapists work with clients who have mental, emotional, or behavioral disorders, providing psychotherapy, behavior modification, and other forms of treatment. *Social psychologists* make use of psychology, sociology, and cultural anthropology to study different ways individuals and groups interact. *Developmental psychologists* study the way behavior changes from infancy through old age. *School psychologists* work with children, teachers, parents, and administrators to treat children's learning and behavioral problems. *Experimental psychologists* do research on human and animal behavior, studying such areas as learning and retention, sensory processes, and the effects of substance abuse.

Licensing as a clinical or counseling psychologist requires a Ph.D. in psychology, successful completion of an approved internship, and a year or two of professional experience. The average starting salary for a clinical, counseling, or research psychologist is $40,000 per year; for school psychologists, $45,000. The average salary for all psychologists with doctorates is $65,000 per year.

Veterinarian

Veterinarians care for pets, livestock, and sporting and laboratory animals, and they protect the public from exposure to animal diseases. Typically veterinarians diagnose medical problems, dress wounds, set broken bones, perform surgery, and prescribe and administer medicines and vaccines. Most veterinarians are in private practice. The majority treat small animals such as dogs, cats, and birds. Others concentrate on larger animals or have a mixed practice for both large and small animals.

Working as a Mental Health Technician

One of the most critical health care problems in our society is alcohol and drug addiction. There is much confusion about the nature of addiction. Most medical practitioners agree that alcoholism and other forms of addiction are diseases and must be treated. However, the laws of most states make the possession of drugs a crime, and being intoxicated a crime when driving a vehicle. Because of the blame and shame associated with addictions, treatment centers operate under strict codes of confidentiality.

The state of California recently passed legislation that emphasizes treatment, rather than jail sentences, for addiction-related crimes. The new laws give drug and alcohol offenders the option of going to a treatment facility. In Port Hueneme, California, Jaime is a mental health technician working at a residential facility. The term "residential" means that while the patients are closely supervised, they are not locked in.

Jaime has lived in California all his life. His mother grew up in New Mexico and his father in Texas, but they settled on the California coast in a small town north of Santa Barbara before Jaime was born. He grew up bilingual because his parents always spoke Spanish at home.

Like many of the mental health technicians working in treatment centers, one of Jaime's qualifications for the job was his own successful recovery process. He can honestly say, "Been there, done that."

One of the most important aspects of Jaime's job is providing a positive role model. He is living proof that with courage and determination, recovery from addiction is possible.

Graduation from an accredited college of veterinary medicine and a license to practice are required. Licensing is controlled by the states. Competition for admission to vet school is keen. Candidates must have a significant number of undergraduate credits in math and science or a bachelor of science degree. Those admitted to vet college usually have a grade point average of 3.0 or better. The growth rate of this field is faster than average. Earnings rise significantly as veterinarians gain experience. A beginning vet would start out at about $30,000. Median income is $51,000, and the top 10 percent earn $106,000 or more per year.

PART 2

Profiles of Success

· · · · · · · · · · · · · · · · **TABLE OF CONTENTS** · · · · · · · · · · · · · · · ·

Dr. Juana Acrivos—Professor of Chemistry
(California)   37

José Alonso, Jr.—Physicist (Florida)   43

Dr. Pedro Barbosa—Entomologist
(Maryland)   51

Dr. Isabel Dominguez—Geneticist
(Massachusetts)   57

Dr. Fidel Hernandez—Zoologist (Texas) 63

Dr. Theresa Ortega—Veterinarian
(California)   69

Dr. Eloy Rodriguez—Toxicologist (Texas) 75

Dr. Richard Tapia—Professor of Applied
Mathematics (Texas)   81

Juana Vivó Acrivos

Professor of Chemistry, San José State University

When the energy crisis hit California in the winter of 2001, Dr. Juana Acrivos was already doing research on solid-state chemistry that would be very useful in finding a solution. At San José State College, Dr. Acrivos was working on the superconductivity of layer compounds. A superconductor is a material that carries electricity without resistance. The power shortages in California were not helped by the fact that there is a big loss of electricity between where the power is generated and where it is used. The power lines that we see along the roads are not efficient carriers of electricity because they have too much resistance, and resistance causes energy loss. In addition, repeated temperature changes from day to night increase the loss. If the existing lines, which are usually made of aluminum or copper, were to be replaced by superconductors, more power could be delivered to areas that need it.

Dr. Acrivos started her work on superconductors in the 1970s while she was on sabbatical at the Cavendish Laboratories in Cambridge, England. A sabbatical is a paid leave from one's regular job, during which one has the opportunity to work or study somewhere else. In Cambridge she began working on layer compounds, which are two-dimensional and make very good conductors.

An example of a layer compound that everyone is familiar with is graphite, the material in pencil lead. Graphite is a two-dimensional material because its electrons move backward and forward and side to side, but not up and down. This means that its layers slide easily over each other, which is why the dark marks a pencil makes slide onto the paper when we write. For the same reason, graphite is used for lubricating. In the winter you don't want to lubricate locks with oil because oil freezes. If you have trouble with a key sticking in a lock, rub the key with a pencil, and the graphite will make it slip into the lock easily. You can also use the lead of a graphite pencil to improve an electrical contact, especially in hi-fi equipment. So even though a pencil is a three-dimensional object, graphite is considered two-dimensional.

The work Dr. Acrivos does in her laboratory is mostly computation and spectroscopy, which is analyzing materials (prepared by colleagues at Purdue University and at the Cavendish Laboratory) from their spectra. She uses X-ray absorption spectroscopy to look at each element in a material separately. The light she uses can't be obtained from an ordinary light bulb. It has to come from a synchrotron source, something that produces very powerful energy. There is a synchrotron at Stanford that she uses, and there's one in Berkeley. There is also one in England.

"What happens," Dr. Acrivos explains, "at the end of a linear particle accelerator, electrons, and sometimes protons, are bent by powerful magnets. In the process of bending, they give off a broad spectrum of energy. This energy is absorbed in a unique fashion by the individual atoms in the material, which allows for their identification and the determination of their properties. The higher the atomic number (which is equal to the total number of electrons in a neutral atom), the higher the energy that is absorbed by its electrons in a given shell to move to other states. This is what constitutes an X-ray absorption spectrum, where the absorption from each element is very far from another one." Using this very sophisticated process, she can analyze elements to see which ones would be the best conductor, and under what circumstances.

Juana Vivó was born in Havana, Cuba, on June 24, 1928. Her mother, Lilia Azpeitia, was born in Key West, Florida, of Cuban parents, so she was a United States citizen. Cubans have been commuting to Florida for a very long time. The family originally moved to Florida because they were involved in the Cuban War of Independence against Spain in the 19th century. Juana's great-grandmother had fallen in love with a Spanish physician, so they married and went to Florida to be on neutral territory. On her mother's side of the family, most of Juana's relatives were teachers: Another great-grandfather (the founder of San Carlos School in Key West), her mother, and her sister were all teachers.

Juana's father, Adolfo Vivó, came from the province of Matanzas to Havana. There he met General William Pew of Massachusetts, who had gone to Cuba in 1898 to fight in the war of independence. General Pew, who was a bachelor, wanted to adopt the young Adolpho, but the Vivó family wouldn't allow it. Nonetheless the general kept in touch with the Vivó family all his life. Juana still has his medals from the Cuban War of Independence.

"So that's my side of the family," Juana says. "Very Cuban. As a matter of fact, when I became a U.S. citizen, my mother was very upset with me. I just said, 'Well, you gave up your U.S. citizenship, I'm picking it up now.'"

Growing up in Havana, Juana Vivó went to an American Episcopalian school first, then to a public high school. She reports that her preparation was extremely good. She took calculus her last year in high school, and then took physics and chemistry and mathematics in college. She received her doctor of science degree from the University of Havana, and then earned a fellowship to attend the University of Minnesota.

When Juana arrived at the University of Minnesota, the graduate faculty didn't quite know what to do with her. They weren't used to having Latinos in their graduate school science programs, and they weren't used to having women there, either. They looked at her, she says, as though they were thinking, "Are you prepared or not?" Then they told her to take undergraduate courses. "I was skimming through them, making straight As," she remembers. "I noticed that fellows coming from Cal Tech were not doing as well as I was. I realized that my math background was very strong. My math and my physics were extremely strong. We had very little instrumentation in Cuba, but we were strong on theory.

"If you have brains, you can get theory anywhere. And that's what I see is going to be good for developing countries, because theory can be learned without expensive instrumentation. And in this age of fast computer communications, anything is possible for young kids from any country. . . . Theory can be taught anyplace there is electrical power to run a fast communications system, providing the kids want to learn."

Juana went to the University of Minnesota in 1951. She was the only girl in the class. One of her classmates there was Andreas Acrivos, a Greek student she would later marry. Years after she and Andreas were married, another classmate told her a story that astonished her: "When I came into the class in Minnesota," Juana remembers, "I was all bundled up and I had to take off my scarf, my coat, my gloves, my hat. And these—whatever you want to call them—these young men made bets on the number of clothes I would take off. It's funny now, but can you imagine me knowing that they were counting the number of clothes I would take off?"

Juana was the top student in her class. After the initial resistance and astonishment she encountered because she was a Latina, she smiled and won them over with her high grades. She thinks perhaps that because she was scared, coming from Cuba and being so far from home, she studied more than the others did. After her fellowship expired, they asked her to stay to finish her Ph.D., and the University of Minnesota supported her.

Juana Vivó got her Ph.D. in 1956, and she and Andreas went to Cuba so that he could meet her family. They were married there and then moved to Berkeley, California, where Andreas had a teaching job. "I came to Berkeley and had to look for a job," Juana remembers, "but I didn't have a driver's license. So of course I had to learn to drive." She got a position doing postdoctoral research at Stanford University. Once she learned how to drive, she made the long commute from Berkeley to Stanford for two years. Then she decided to take another postdoctoral position at Berkeley. Two years later, her husband received an offer from Stanford.

"So we went," she says. "San José State College, which is close to Stanford, was just beginning to emphasize a strong science curriculum. I wanted to teach, so I went there in 1962." San José was a very small school, the department was not known, and when she applied to the National Science Foundation for support, the referees apparently said, "What kind of research can she do at that school?" Juana had to work hard, and she had to fight. Her first proposal was approved in 1966. She started a process that has been much copied since: teaching undergraduate students to do research so that when they get to graduate school, they are in a tremendous position to be advanced. More than 90 percent of her undergraduate research students have gone on to get their Ph.D.'s.

"My students have done very well," Dr. Acrivos says. "I have professors at universities all over the world. I've kept in touch. On Christmas Eve of 2000 I had a letter from a professor of neurology at the University of Pennsylvania, asking me if I remembered him. Of course I remembered him! This was from 1967."

In the spring of 2000, after years of teaching courses in physical chemistry, quantum mechanics, and chemical computation at San José State, Dr. Juana Vivó Acrivos became professor emerita. While teaching there she was four times awarded the university's Meritorious Professional Performance Award. She had taken several sabbaticals to Cambridge, England—to Trinity College in 1984 and to Cavendish College in 1991. Her research has been funded by the National Science Foundation, the IBM Corporation, and the William M. Keck Foundation. She has over 100 journal publications, coauthored with her graduate and undergraduate students.

Now that she is a professor emerita, which basically means that she has retired with full academic privileges, she is concentrating on her research. "At the moment I have some graduate students," she says, "but I'll be working with postdoctorals from now on because I'm retired. I still have three graduate students who are working with me. I love teaching and know by experience that good research is essential to good teaching. I've been doing research part-time, and now I'm doing research full-time. It's not just doing the experiment, it's thinking about the results and thinking about what to apply these things to."

Dr. Juana Acrivos's research is currently challenged by something called nano materials. A string of several carbon atoms the size of several nanometers is called a nano tube. A nanometer is one billionth of a meter. These tiny, tiny wires can be used to carry electricity. She thinks they can also be made with the layer compounds she is researching. "I have a proposal to the National Science Foundation for doing applied works with these two-dimensional materials to make batteries," she says. "There are no nano batteries yet. . . . We're looking at these things, and this proposal I wrote last summer was when we weren't aware of the power crunch. We now know that this will be useful."

The shy Cuban girl who braved the cold Minnesota winter and her rowdy male classmates half a century ago has had a sure instinct for being useful. Not only did she demonstrate that she could survive and excel in the academic world, she did far more than that. With her commitment to teaching she has prepared other scientists to excel, and with her research she is continuing to keep the lights on for all of us.

José Alonso, Jr.

Physicist, NASA (National Aeronautics and Space Administration)

On Wednesday, February 7, 2001, the space shuttle *Atlantis* was launched from NASA's Kennedy Space Center. It carried the biggest payload ever, the $1.4 billion, 30,000-pound Destiny space laboratory. On that day and the following days, the world's newspapers, radios, and televisions reported news of the shuttle's successful docking with the International Space Station *Alpha*. When the mission was successfully completed, one newspaper article reported: "Thanks to the *Atlantis* astronauts, Alpha now has a fourth room—the $1.4 billion Destiny laboratory. It took all five crew members and three space walks to install the lab module."

That was the most dramatic part—and certainly the bravery and skill of the astronauts is worthy of celebration. But hundreds of other dedicated scientists and technicians had been working for over two years at Kennedy Space Center getting the lab ready for its historic delivery to the space station. One of these scientists is physicist José Alonso, Jr.

"We perform two primary functions here at KSC," José Alonso says. "We prepare the launch vehicles (shuttles, Delta rockets, etc.) for launch, and we also perform the final checkouts and integration of the payloads to their designated launch vehicles." The payloads are those items the launch vehicles carry to orbit, such as the huge Destiny space laboratory or a satellite being launched by a Delta rocket. At Kennedy Space Center, the customers such as the Boeing Company or its subsidiary Rocketdyne are provided with facilities to check out their payloads. The KSC NASA space station processing crew also does their own check outs, putting the various segments together to be sure that everything fits prior to launching the components for assembly in orbit.

The lab is a development of Marshall Space Flight Center. It came to Kennedy Space Center in 1998, before it was completed. "[The lab] was one of the elements that we [tested] with the other segments, making sure that it was going to communicate and interface with the other segments that are going up to the space station in the future, and some segments that went up before," José Alonso explains. "And basically this lab is the real cornerstone of the space station, at least for some time in the future. It contains most of the capability for performing science and communications with the other segments.

"My job was to provide support to the people who were actually doing the checkouts. So if they needed spares, they had the spares in time to perform the various scheduled functions. We also made and repaired parts and pieces in support of the flight hardware processing, which took place on the Space Station Processing Facility high bay floor. Basically, my organization dealt with providing the interface between the people on the floor who were actually doing the work, the hands-on work, and the logistics infrastructure here at Kennedy Space Center."

The laboratory is now a functioning part of the space station. It is a scientific environment that also has a lot of controls over station-wide systems, such as the power system. With electricity generated by giant solar wings, its computers are running fuel-free attitude-control gyroscopes, which took over control from the expensive fuel-guzzling Russian thrusters.

The main purpose of the space station is space exploration, which means learning how to live in space. Scientists will be doing research in the environment of a complete vacuum, which may result in new technologies or capabilities that we haven't even guessed at yet. "At the same time," Mr. Alonso says, "we're learning how to live in space, how to survive in space so that we can in the future—ten years, fifteen years down the road—have the experience of living in space. We'll be deciding—and I hope it doesn't take fifteen years—whether we will send people to Mars. How do you send someone to Mars if we don't know how to live in space?"

José Alonso was born in Tampa, Florida, on November 10, 1944. Both his parents were also born in Tampa, of immigrant parents. José's grandparents on his father's side came from Spain; his mother's parents were Cuban. All had been drawn to Tampa by the thriving cigar industry there— at the turn of the last century, cigars were the biggest industry in Florida. There was a very large Hispanic community that grew up around Tampa's cigar industry.

As he was growing up, José knew few people who were actually from Cuba themselves. Most were second- or third-generation Americans of Cuban, Spanish, or Italian background, although the subculture was primarily a Cuban subculture. He remembers, "The black beans and the rice and the roast pork for New Year's and Christmas Eve celebrations—although we were Americans, a lot of the customs that we celebrated were Cuban. Everywhere you went you spoke Spanish. Spanish was the language of the cigar industry in Tampa.

"Even though we shared a lot in the way of cultural things, and common language, there were some differences in the way the people were. Tampa Latins were different than Cubans in the way they saw things, the way they treated their women, politial views, etc. Even though it was a Latin community, it was still an American community."

José's mother and father spoke Spanish at home, and José grew up bilingual. He doesn't remember learning either English or Spanish, but he isn't as fluent at reading Spanish as he is English. He didn't start taking Spanish classes until he was in junior high school, and thinks the studying of Spanish is something we should emphasize much more in our schools. "My wife and I are both bilingual," he says, "but because we were educated in English and we didn't live in a Hispanic community like Tampa's Ybor City district, our kids know even less Spanish than we do. Much less. In my wife's case, her mother and father were both bilingual Tampa people like we were, but they were better educated than my parents were. They had high school educations."

José's stepfather, whose education ended at the fourth or fifth grade, owned a Cuban bread bakery. "He could read English. I remember he used to read the newspaper," José says. "I don't think he could read Spanish. He never was educated in Spanish. My mother went up to the seventh grade, and she could read English, too."

José has a brother two years younger than he is, and a sister five years younger. His stepfather's bakery was a successful business, making Cuban bread for the sandwich shops and restaurants in the Hispanic district of Tampa. "We never lacked for anything growing up," he remembers. "I had a car when I was sixteen."

He went to a private elementary school, a Methodist school that he remembers as being quite good. "The public schools probably were not that good," he says, "probably below average. Outside of what I learned in elementary school, I don't believe that I learned that much more. Of course, my attitude toward education might have been a problem back then."

José was always good at math, and other areas as well. For a short time the family lived in Jacksonville, Florida, when he was in the first or second grade. He remembers that the teacher would have him read out loud to the class to show them how it should be done. "When you're the new kid, that isn't always the best thing," he says. He also used to excel in the spelling bees they had at school.

Jose dropped out of Jefferson High School in Tampa in 1962 and joined the U.S. Army for three years. The army accepted him on the stipulation that he continue his education while serving and obtain a GED, which he did. When he got out of the army in 1965, he was thinking seriously about what sort of career he would have. His first attempt to prepare himself for the working world was taking a technical program in drafting. "That was one whole year of sitting in a classroom six hours a day drafting. I got a certificate that I was a draftsman. Even after I did that and was working as a draftsman, I was still working for minimum wage. So I thought I needed more education."

His next attempt at more education took him to St. Petersburg Junior College. His time in the army qualified him for college benefits under the GI Bill, so he started out in a two-year mechanical technology program. Besides the technical classes, requirements included taking a lot of mathematics—algebra and calculus— and physics.

"I didn't have any intentions of even getting a bachelor's degree then," José remembers. "I noticed that in my physics classes, I did better than anybody else in the class. In fact I remember one exam when the professor gave a problem on the exam that he couldn't solve. I could. He didn't count it for the rest of the class, but he let me keep the credit. That's when I realized, hey, maybe I have a knack for this physics."

When José neared the end of the mechanical technology program, he realized he was doing very well and that it would be a good idea to stay in school and get a bachelor's degree. The next problem he had to solve was what to major in. He considered electrical engineering, mechanical engineering, physics, and chemistry. To help him make a decision, he went out to Kennedy Space Center to talk to several personnel departments and find out what kind of people they liked to hire.

One of the things that emerged from his discussion with the personnel people at Kennedy was that they liked physics majors because of their science background. Physics majors could be trained to fit into just about any position. "That fit me just fine because I did well in physics," José says. He decided to major in physics to give himself a lot of flexibility in the jobs he could apply for when he graduated.

"I didn't know," he says. "It's not like I was exposed to a lot of people who had physics careers, or engineering careers. The people I grew up around were primarily businesspeople, people who owned their own businesses. And even though many of them were not well educated, it wasn't that they were stupid. There just wasn't a lot of education in the environment, so I wasn't exposed to what the lifestyle of an engineer was, or what the lifestyle of a physicist would be. I kind of made my way, taking into consideration what came to me the best, in terms of what I liked."

He transferred to the University of South Florida in Tampa, into the physics department. He set a course for a bachelor of arts in physics because the arts degree would allow him to take other classes that he enjoyed. He took business, anthropology, and philosophy classes as well as science classes, and says, "I think I got a better, well-rounded education with a B.A." He completed the degree in 1971.

After he graduated, he interviewed with NASA and was offered a position. He also interviewed with three private companies and was offered a position with each of those. He accepted the NASA position at Goddard. By that time he was married—he had gotten married in 1967, during his second semester at junior college, to a Tampa girl who had been a friend of his sister's. He and his wife, Sandra, have three children, two boys and a girl, and three grandchildren so far.

José Alonso has been at NASA ever since 1971. He spent two years at Goddard, then took a leave of absence to go to graduate school. He returned to South Florida in Tampa, and while he was there getting a master's degree in physics, he remembered that Kennedy Space Center was close by. He went to Kennedy to explore the possibility of transferring there from

Goddard, and he did. It was closer to home, and it was where the action was in the space program.

He was at Kennedy in 1975 when they made the linkup between the Russians and Americans (Apollo-Soyuz program) in space. "The American segment was launched on a Saturn vehicle," he remembers, "the last Saturn vehicle that we launched. The one that we used to send men to the moon during the Apollo program. I was able to see the last Saturn vehicle launched."

Mr. Alonso says that times have changed a lot since the cold war years when the Russians and Americans "competed to see who was going to be the biggest and baddest guy on the block in respect to space flight. . . . It was a very costly competition. I've heard estimates as high as a hundred billion dollars were spent on the Apollo program. Today's space program environment is very cost-conscious. We're moving forward toward our long-range goals in well-planned steps rather than in one fell swoop as during the Apollo program."

Right now one of NASA's long-range exploration goals is to send astronauts to Mars to explore the planet. Currently spacecraft are being sent to Mars to gather information about the environment and the terrain and perhaps to set up a satellite communications system around Mars so that we'd be able to communicate with people when we send them.

What José Alonso likes best about his job is the fact that he's taking part in the development of something special. "There's something very special that I feel I'm able to contribute to this thing. Not only to the American people, but to mankind as a whole."

People get hired to work for NASA at about $30,000 per year. Mr. Alonso says that within five or six years, "depending on how aggressive you are and how lucky you are in the positions you're able to move into, you can move up to $50,000. The ratings go up to $112,000 a year."

His advice to young people who are thinking about what career they would like to have is to follow what they like, keeping in mind that they will use this education to earn a living. "And to remember that they live in a country where, I don't care what your economic background is, if you want to accomplish something, you can accomplish it. Many people do not take advantage of living in a country with as many opportunities as we have available to us. Set your goals high and work hard at achieving them—I would wager that everyone that takes advantage of the opportunities available to them would surpass their goals way beyond their wildest dreams.

As a high school dropout entering the army at seventeen years of age, I would never have imagined that someday I would be a physicist helping to build a space station."

Dr. Pedro Barbosa

Entomologist, University of Maryland

Pedro Barbosa III was born in Guayama, Puerto Rico, in 1944. His parents, who both had third-grade educations, moved to New York City when he was three years old. They settled in Spanish Harlem, where Pedro grew up. His mother, Magdalena, worked as a seamstress in the lower Manhattan garment district, and his father, Pedro Barbosa Jr., had a series of odd jobs. Although he had a half-brother, Pedro grew up as an only child. The only language spoken at home was Spanish, and there was a lot of Spanish in his environment.

Because both of his parents worked, Pedro was placed in a preschool program where he quickly learned English, so he grew up bilingual. "I guess I learned to read in Spanish," he says, "because I can read [Spanish] now. I'm not sure how. I did take some Spanish classes in college, but not many because I hadn't learned the grammar. I could read Spanish before I went to college, but I don't know how that happened because my parents didn't read newspapers, and there weren't very many books around."

What he does remember is the influence of his uncle, his father's brother, who was interested in science. His uncle lived nearby and frequently came over. Although he had wanted to be a doctor, Pedro's uncle worked as a nurses' aide. "I think he was sort of doing things vicariously," Pedro remembers. "He talked a lot about science. He'd cut out articles, he'd talk about science and medicine. He got me an encyclopedia, and would buy books and bring them home. So he was probably the one who motivated my general interest in science. Originally when I went to college, I went thinking I wanted to be a doctor. Which was not true."

The public schools in Spanish Harlem were not very good. When it was time for him to go to high school, Pedro wanted to go to one of the two magnet schools that specialized in science, Stuyvesant High School or the Bronx High School of Science. Unfortunately he couldn't pass the exam required for entrance to those schools. Instead he went to Charles Evans Hughes High School, which had a joint program in engineering and science.

Pedro Barbosa graduated from high school in 1962. At that time, New York had a program in which any high school graduate with a B average could go to college. The only cost was a $27 fee per semester. Pedro had a B average because expectations were low in the high school he attended. "So B wasn't hard to do," he remembers. "I also had half a scholarship to a university, but we couldn't come up with the other $1,500, so it didn't make any difference."

He went to City College of New York, a commuter college where there was no sense of community or much involvement with other students. While he was there, he worked in a haberdashery downtown. It was a small store, just a man and his wife and Pedro. He started out as a salesclerk, but after a while the couple who owned the store would go on vacation and leave him in charge. The relationship he had with them, and their trust and respect, helped him build up confidence in himself.

He needed that confidence to get through his undergraduate courses at City College. Because of the poor preparation he had in high school, he

had a lot of difficulties. He had no foundation in math. He failed physics twice before he finally passed. "That's why I had a horrible grade point average," he says, "because I was learning everything from scratch. I just struggled to learn enough to keep moving on. . . . As an undergraduate, very little was relevant to me. I failed a lot of courses."

In the process of struggling through college, he found his passion: "When I could take biology, that's what I loved. When I went to City College I took every biology course I could. I took fifty-one credits of biology, and I loved it. . . . I got a mixture of As and Bs, mostly As. My cumulative was still C-minus, but I loved biology and I had some wonderful teachers. Now that I'm an entomologist, I've learned that three of them were world-renowned entomologists."

Pedro Barbosa earned a B.S. in biology in 1966. He applied to a lot of graduate schools . . . and got rejected by a lot of graduate schools. Finally he was accepted by three schools; one of them accepted him on probation, and that was the one he selected: the University of Massachusetts in Amherst.

"I was very lucky," he says. "I made the decision on very unacademic criteria, but it was a perfect decision. . . It made a tremendous difference in my ability to succeed. I was street-smart and world-stupid for a variety of reasons—because of my background, and because I was a New Yorker. New Yorkers never think there's any world outside of New York. Everything was new to me. I was impressed by seeing a corn plant, or cows. Those were very weird, unusual things for me. It was not a world I was exposed to before."

Barbosa found that the University of Massachusetts graduate school had a great sense of community. The entomology department was small but was run by very distinguished people. It was well on its way to being one of the best departments in the Northeast. His adviser had been on the job for only about a year and was extremely supportive. "Indeed," Dr. Barbosa says, "what I have learned in retrospect is that the most important thing to do with minority students—and it often isn't done for benign reasons—is not to lower expectations. In fact, what my adviser did was put on expectations that were higher than normal. But since I had no clue, I assumed they were normal. I went ahead and did it."

Dr. Barbosa says that his academic life had always been one of being the only minority student, or of being with only one or two others at most. He attended City College of New York well before it had a significant enrollment of Latino students. So being the only minority student in the graduate program in entomology at the University of Massachusetts was nothing new for him. It was what he was used to, so it didn't bother him.

He says that scholastic life became easier the further he went: "College was extremely difficult, masters' graduate school was easier; and earning the Ph.D. was basically a piece of cake. For many reasons, the introductory courses are much harder than advanced courses, even for an undergraduate. You're learning the basics of everything—like math builds on what you know, so it's extremely difficult. You go on, if you have a passion for what you're doing—which is absolutely critical."

Dr. Barbosa got his master's degree and continued, earning his Ph.D. in 1971. He met the woman who would become his wife, Gail, while he was at the University of Massachusetts, but when he finished his Ph.D. and got a job, they parted because neither of them believed in the institution of marriage. It was the early 1970s, after all, when young people despised all institutions, didn't trust anyone over thirty, and imagined that love could be free.

After beginning his first job, at Rutgers University, Pedro Barbosa changed his mind about a number of things, chief among them marriage. He and Gail were married and had two boys and two girls. She chose to stay at home with their children and support him in his career until the children were grown and on their own.

In his career, Pedro made a change of specialization when he got to Rutgers. He had done his doctoral work with mosquitoes, but Rutgers had many people working with mosquitoes. "I thought it would be wise for me to alter my path," he remembers. "There were too many people doing the same thing. It didn't seem to be a good idea—I was an assistant professor."

Dr. Barbosa's specialty is ecology, which is what he is researching now at the University of Maryland, where some of the entomologists are physiologists and some are molecular biologists, but all are focused on insects. Their mission is to come up with ideas or research that could ultimately be applied to the regulation of pests. One of the side benefits of his job is the chance to travel, since pest control is a vital issue all over the world.

His days vary quite a bit, which he says is part of the fun. The days that are devoted to research could involve a variety of things: taking data from previous experiments, writing the articles that will report the results of the research, or writing grants to get funding for new ideas for research. He may go out into the field, or he may be in the laboratory setting up and starting experiments. He may meet with graduate students who are doing research that they have agreed and decided upon together. He also supervises a number of people in technical support positions and may talk with them about the progress of research he has planned and developed.

Depending on the time of year, Dr. Barbosa may work with undergraduates or sometimes with high school students. "I try to do as much as I can to expose students to research, particularly minority students. There are a variety of different programs. There are institutions near here, like the U.S. Department of Agriculture, that have internships for students. My university has programs that bring in high school students just so they can see another Latino person doing research."

For most minority students, Dr. Barbosa says, their exposure to biology is almost always medicine, dentistry, and sometimes pharmacy. This is in part because most high school biology is very molecular and health oriented, so they never know there's another whole world out there, the world of scientific research.

For several years Dr. Barbosa's interest has been in looking at the ecology, the interconnections between plants, the insects that feed on the plants, and the parasitic insects that feed on the insects that feed on plants. What the researchers were doing was looking at the chemistry of the plants and how it affected the herbivores (insects that eat the plants) and their parasites.

"We can increase biological control by using a parasite that is adapted by breeding before we release it," Dr. Barbosa says. "The parasite will be more effective in attacking the insect that is eating a particular crop. Increasing the biological control this way will make people less likely to use dangerous pesticides to kill the destructive insects."

In addition to his research, Dr. Barbosa also teaches at the University of Maryland. He says that there are no real drawbacks to his job, only things that he does that are more fun than other things. "The only bad part about teaching," he says, "is that it's very hard. It never gets easier. Research is very easy, predictable, has a beginning point and end point, but teaching changes every time the group changes. But it is definitely fun. Actually the most important part of the job of research is working with students. It's the quality part of the job."

When asked for his advice to young people, he mentions three things that he feels are most important. The first is to find something you have a passion for and "go for it, because that is what will determine how happy you are." The second is to enjoy the process of what you are doing rather than counting on the goals, because "the goal is ephemeral, but the process you can keep." And finally, to experience as much of the world as you can, "to keep balanced because it makes you grow as a person."

Dr. Isabel Dominguez

Geneticist, Harvard Medical School

Dr. Isabel Dominguez was born on November 27, 1965, in Baracaldo, Spain, and moved to nearby Bilbao when she was two years old. She earned her Ph.D. in her native country in 1994 and came to the United States to do postdoctoral studies at Harvard Medical School. She's been at Harvard ever since, doing research in genetics. Dr. Dominguez is interested in understanding how the frog embryo develops.

"There are many things that are interesting about embryo development," she says. "One is just how it happens. When you look at it, it's almost a miracle. From an egg and sperm you get a living being. . . . Studying it is just wonderful."

Many of the processes that happen in humans during development can also be found in mice, frogs, and other living creatures. Using frogs, chicks, flies, worms, or other animal models, geneticists can study the genes that participate in these different processes. These studies can help scientists understand what happens in the development of the human embryo and catch early genetic problems.

This is a story of passion—a passion to understand the miracle of life. Isabel Dominguez grew up in a house full of singing birds. In Bilbao, in the beautiful Basque country of northern Spain, her father, Teofilo, was a metalworker in a factory, but at home he bred and raised canaries and sheltered many other animals—dogs and cats and rabbits. When she was a child, Isabel watched in amazement as the tiny canary chicks emerged from the shells of their delicate eggs.

Isabel and her two younger sisters, Belen and Yolanda, went to public schools in Bilbao. Isabel loved mathematics—for a while she wanted to be a mathematician—and, unlike some, never considered for a moment that it was something a girl couldn't be good at. She was good at it. Math and science were important to her, not clothes and makeup and boys. This was a bit of a disappointment to her mother, Agustina, a homemaker and part-time janitor, who would have liked to have dressed her daughter in pretty clothes, but Isabel simply wasn't interested.

Isabel went to public high school, where the focus of her attention turned from mathematics to chemistry, and she planned to be a chemist. Then, as though she were following a plan of development as mysterious as the process by which cells divide and specialize from a single fertilized egg, her interests drew her to biology.

After high school, Isabel went to the University of the Basque Country, commuting the 15 kilometers (9 miles) from her home in Bilbao to the campus. Because her family had a relatively low income and her grades were high, Isabel attended the university on government grants that paid for her tuition, books, and supplies.

Isabel Dominguez earned her bachelor's and master's degrees at the University of the Basque Country and then followed Dr. Jorge Moscat to the Autonoma University in Madrid. She was fascinated by Dr. Moscat's work with oncogenes, genes whose mutations result in cancer. Her work in his lab in Madrid led to the questions she is still asking, and trying to answer, about how the cells in developing embryos know what course to take. What messages do cells receive that tell them whether to be an eye or a thighbone? How do cells receive these messages and interpret them?

Isabel earned her Ph.D. from Autonoma University in 1994. Only two weeks later she traveled to the United States to work as a postdoctoral geneticist in the research laboratories of Harvard Medical School, a position she still holds. Salaries for postdoctoral researchers usually start around $28,000 per year for academic research, and increase depending on the number of years of experience. The National Institutes of Health set the guidelines for doctoral fellows' salaries. Isabel has worked in Beth Israel Hospital with Dr. Sergei Sokol and now is in the Dana Farber Cancer Institute with Dr. Jeremy Green.

Dr. Dominguez says that the life of a postdoctoral research fellow is exciting because of the possibility of finding new genes. "Not only finding them," she says, "but finding out how they work and how that will lead to development. That's the most exciting part. As a benefit of working with frogs, you can see how they develop in front of your eyes from the very beginning, and it's absolutely amazing. You can see the cells dividing, the embryo elongating, developing eyes, muscles."

Research also requires long hours in the lab. On many days Isabel arrives in the lab between 8:00 and 9:00 A.M. If she is working with embryos, she will take the eggs the frog has laid and fertilize them. She looks to see that they are fine and waits for them to start dividing. She may inject them if the experiment requires it, and then look at how they develop, making sure that they are viable. Then she will look at what she gets after she manipulates them. Sometimes the experiments take a long time. The earliest she goes home is about 7:00 P.M. The latest is whenever the experiment is finished, which could be into the small hours of the next morning.

Once she has begun a research project, Isabel sets her own hours, her own work pace. Before that, the project is discussed with her adviser, who makes suggestions about the procedures. Her adviser will monitor the experiments, and she will report on her progress, but for the most part Isabel sets her own schedule. After she begins collecting data, the entire lab team will comment on and criticize it. "That is part of the growing process in a project," she says. "Many people input their criticisms and also their ideas. At the end of all this

process you will get, hopefully, an answer to what you were looking for."

When asked what skills or talents are necessary for this field, Isabel said that you have to have the ability to ask a question about something you are interested in. Then you should be able to think about possibilities and hypotheses, perform and analyze your experiments, discuss the results and think about where they are going. You have to be able to connect your work with the work from other research that has been published already. Finally, you have to be skilled with your hands and be able to work with animals or cells. "You really have to be fascinated about this," she says, "because it's a job that takes most of your day, your time, not nine to five. It's mentally exhausting sometimes. . . . Sometimes a discovery takes a long time, so you really have to be strong to be able to continue and continue and continue despite bad results or wrong results or the time it takes to develop a particular technique."

Developing effective techniques is a major part of the job of a postdoctoral fellow in research. The things Isabel works with are very, very small. A frog is small, a frog embryo smaller still. And the single fertilized cell from which the embryo begins to grow is very, very small indeed. To learn how to inject something into these very small bits of living tissue takes a lot of concentration and practice. Mapping the sequence of the genes in the chromosomes is another painstaking process. "Once you can identify the sequence of genes," Isabel says, "you can see if the sequence is correct or if it has a mutation that may lead to a disease in people."

When she thinks about the future, Isabel Dominguez is not sure where her path will lead her. She knows that she likes to teach and feels she has been effective in the labs where she has worked, teaching the techniques she has learned to others. Continuing in the academic world as a teacher is one of the possibilities open to her. Another possibility is accepting a position in industry where salaries can be very high. But her first love is research. "I would prefer to work full-time in research," she says, "because that's what drives me. But explaining things to other people is also really gratifying."

For Isabel Dominguez, the long hours required are worth it, but she thinks that they can be a problem for women with families. "If you are a mother, it can be really difficult," she says. "Not that it is impossible. There

are women who are absolutely amazing. They can cope with having kids and maintain their positions as advisers in the university. They really deserve a lot of credit. You're pushed to have a lot of results, and sometimes it is difficult to balance your personal life and your scientific life."

Isabel's passion for all aspects of life helps her keep that balance. She has many hobbies. She likes drawing and painting and has worked with stained glass. She's learning how to sail and how to ice skate, which she never did in Spain because it wasn't cold enough. She loves hiking and going to movies and the theater with friends. And she finds that New England is a good place to learn about the history of the United States.

When asked what she thought were the keys to her success, Isabel said that part of it was having had really great teachers, from school to university, and really good mentors afterward in her doctoral and postdoctoral studies. "The second part is a family that really supported me," she says. "That is key, having somebody who really believes in you." The third factor has been her interest in what she is doing: "I like to discover new things and find out what is behind how cells behave and how they respond. These three things are the key to my success."

Her advice to young people just starting to take their first steps on the path that will lead to their careers is to listen to their hearts to find what they are passionate about.

"Just do whatever you're passionate about," she says, "because you're going to be happier. If you like plants, you develop to be a botanist or a gardener. And if you like machines, you'll be an engineer or a mechanic, whatever you really like. If you really love teaching kids, you should be a teacher. Whatever you are interested in, hold on to it."

Dr. Isabel Dominguez enjoys a vacation with family.

Fidel Hernandez

Zoologist, Texas A&M University

It's a Saturday, and Fidel Hernandez is running bird dogs through a pasture in south Texas, occasionally flushing coveys of bobwhites. The scene seems familiar enough—some of the boys out hunting—or so anyone watching them would assume. But a lot more is going on out in that field than a casual observer could know.

Even though he seems too young for such a position, Fidel is a professor of zoology, holding a joint appointment with the Caesar Kleberg Wildlife Research Institute. At age 27 he has already earned his Ph.D. and has a teaching appointment with the Department of Animal and Wildlife Sciences at Texas A&M University in Kingsville, Texas. Having a joint appointment means that half his time is spent teaching and half is spent in research. His activities with the English pointers out in the pasture are part of one of his research projects.

The quail in this study are wearing little radio transmitters. The birds were trapped, collared with the device, and released as part of a long-term radio telemetry project on bobwhites. The scientists are collecting ecological information on the population, survival, mortality, and nesting success. On this particular Saturday, Fidel is gathering information about how successful hunting dogs are in finding quail coveys. He knows where the birds are because he has monitoring devices.

The dogs have only their old-fashioned noses to help them find the quail. "We know, for instance, that there are fifty radio-collared coveys out there," Fidel says, "and the dogs only find twenty-five of them. So we get a feel that fifty percent of the coveys are not being detected by the bird dogs. On those particular coveys, we make observations about why that covey wasn't detected."

The scientists not only find out what the bobwhites are doing right, but they also learn what dog handlers may be doing wrong. "If you have an inexperienced driver and he's driving too fast," Fidel says, "the dogs are running and they don't have time to survey the area. And so they miss more coveys. So these are things as far as technique that we can suggest to the researchers that are handling bird dogs. You get a feel for under what conditions dogs are more efficient at locating coveys and provide a better index of what's actually out there."

After lunch at the hunting lodge, Fidel is back out beginning another study, this one on the effects of feeding on nesting ecology. Using a global positioning system that interprets information received from satellites orbiting the earth, Fidel is connecting coordinates on the ground. These will be used, once he sees how they lie in relationship to the land, to set up the bird feeders that will be used in the study.

After two or three hours of laying the groundwork for the feeding study, Fidel and the other researchers turn to a survey of the hawks and other raptors that migrate through Texas. "The southern part of Texas acts as a funnel for a lot of the migration routes for your raptors and tropical migrants and just a lot of your birds," Fidel says. "So we have a huge diversity who pass through here either for the winter migrations or the fall migrations. . . . The peregrine falcon migrates from up in the tundra of North America down to Venezuela in southern South America. As these massive migrations of hawks come through, what effect does it have on the quail that are residents?"

Because the radio transmitters on the quail allow the researchers to monitor their movements, their home range, and their survival, they serve as mortality sensors that tell when the bird hasn't moved for eight hours. If it hasn't moved, it likely is dead. The researchers not only get the numbers, but they can also figure out how the birds were killed. "A hawk will kill it differently than a bobcat or a coyote," Fidel says. "We go look at the mortality site and decide what percentage of kills are hawk kills or mammalian kills. It's a real, real handy technique because it gives you incredible insight as to the ecology of the animal that otherwise you wouldn't have access to just by observation alone."

These south Texas landscapes have been home for Fidel Hernandez his whole life.

He was born in Del Rio, Texas, on March 23, 1972. His parents were born in Rio Grande, Zacatecas, Mexico. His father came over as an illegal worker in the 1960s and then got his green card. Both of Fidel's parents became U.S. citizens after 1995. Fidel's mother had the equivalent of a sixth-grade education in Mexico, and his father finished high school.

"My dad grew up on a ranch in Mexico," Fidel says, "doing the shepherd work with goats and sheep and horses and cattle and all that, and when he came to the U.S., that's the line of work he still works on. He's the foreman for a ranch. And so we grew up helping him there on weekends and during the summer."

Fidel is the sixth and youngest in his family, with three brothers and two sisters. All but one of them graduated from college, and two have master's degrees. His oldest sister, who is now the vice president of a bank, did not go to college. When she got out of high school and was getting ready to go to college, their parents were in a bad auto accident, hit head-on by a drunk driver. Fidel's sister stayed home to take care of the other children while their parents were in the hospital.

Fidel remembers a Saturday night while he was in high school. He and his brothers had wanted to go into town, but at ten o'clock they were still on the ranch working, shipping off steers to the feedlot. "I was tired and hungry and I was out there working, and my dad was out there and my brothers," Fidel remembers. "I think what we had in mind was going out for a night on the town, but since we

were working late we didn't. But anyway, my dad kind of pulled us together, and he said, 'This is why I stress education so much. I expect you all to go to college and get educated because if you don't, here it is Saturday night and instead of being out having a good time, you're here working hard, and if you don't get an education, that's the kind of jobs you're going to get.'"

Fidel's first language is Spanish. His parents didn't know English well enough to read it, and, Fidel says, "I started kindergarten without knowing a lick of English." But although his parents didn't read English, they did read Spanish. After school his dad would have them read Spanish magazines or Spanish fables or other stories so that they could learn how to read the language. Fidel also took Spanish in high school. "It was useful because we already had a strong background and it helped to refine the skills that we already had."

Fidel went to a rural school in Brackettville, Texas, the town nearest the ranch. His 1990 high school graduating class had 37 students, and there were probably only 100 in the whole high school. All of the area's schools—elementary, junior high, and high school—were in buildings on the same lot. But even though the school was small, it had a good math and science program that provided Fidel with a strong foundation for his college work.

After he graduated from high school, Fidel went to Angelo State University. "When I got to college to register, I still remember going through the registration line and they asked me, 'What do you want to major in?' I really didn't have a clue, so some of the advisers started asking me, 'What is your background?' and I started telling them that I grew up on a ranch and they said, 'Well, you sound like you're a biology major, so we'll put you in biology.'"

He says that the advisers that were helping him were biology professors. When you go through the registration process, there are different professors helping the new students. "I always say I was lucky I didn't get a drama or theater arts professor," Fidel says. "I might have been a ballet dancer. I didn't have that inclination toward biology. I never knew that I'd go on to get my Ph.D. and become a professor. I guess the opportunities just arose at the right time and I was at the right place."

While he was at Angelo State, Fidel had an internship at Texas State University, where he worked with faculty members studying bobwhites. He returned to Angelo State enthusiastic about his experience. When he talked about it to his professors, they told him about a professor at Texas A&M who was working with bobwhites. Fidel called, and that turned out to be the professor under whom Fidel would work while earning his master's degree. Their project was studying the nesting ecology of quail and turkey in relation to predators such as raccoon and foxes and bobcats.

Fidel's father had always wanted one of his children to go on to get a Ph.D. As Fidel was completing his master's degree, another project opened up. "I was connected with the right people, so things just fell into my lap, so to speak, throughout my educational career,'" he says. "So I ended up getting my Ph.D. and then got this job. I just graduated in May of 1999, so I'm an assistant professor here. The next step is associate professor and then full professor." The beginning salary for an assistant professor varies from school to school. At Texas A&M, Fidel's starting salary was $45,000 per year for his joint appointment in teaching and research.

Although he emphasizes the good fortune he had in being in the right place at the right time, he also remembers that he worked hard: "I remember in college one Saturday night I was studying organic chemistry—it was after midnight. I was studying with my roommate and I turned around and looked at him and I said, 'What the heck are we doing?' College is supposed to be the most fun of your life and here we are on Saturday night working on chemistry problems.' That just stuck in my mind. Of course it wasn't all work, we did go out some nights and have a night on the town. I just remember that we were constantly trying to do our best to overcome the obstacles."

Dr. Hernandez finds that his bilingual background is very useful in his scientific career. Some of the journals that he publishes in require a Spanish abstract. "A year ago we went to a conference on wildlife conservation in Mexico," he remembers. "Whenever you go down there the biologists don't speak English, so if someone is bilingual like myself, I could just give the presentation in Spanish. It would have a more profound impact on the audience. I do find that having the Spanish background is quite useful.

Particularly in biology, many of the scientific words come from Latin root words. It's much easier to understand the words when you know Spanish."

Fidel Hernandez has many interests. He just bought a house and is starting to enjoy doing repairs and learning woodworking. "I like spending time with my family and friends, visiting my girlfriend. I can devote a Sunday to leisure reading, watching television. . . . Looking back, it was all worth it. Because I went hard at it for about eight years, here I am at twenty-seven as a professor with all the rest of my life ahead of me."

When asked what advice he has for young people who are beginning to think about their career choices, he says, "Don't make excuses as to why you're not in a particular position that you'd like to be in. What I mean by that is, in America, in the United States, how far you get in life is up to you. With perseverance there's enough opportunities out there that you can get as far as you want to. . . . I guess it's a blessing, and a curse at the same time, that most people shoot for mediocrity. It's great for people who have some ambition, because it makes it that much easier for them to shine and really stand out."

Dr. Theresa Ortega

Veterinarian

The Veterinary Medical and Surgical Group facility in Ventura, California, is an intensive care animal hospital equipped with the latest medical technology. Gleaming X-ray and sonogram machines, surgical instruments, a sterile operating theater, and banks of computers are available to assist the specialist veterinary doctors as they care for critically ill animals. These sick pets are referred to the clinic by other veterinarians from all over California and even as far away as Las Vegas, Nevada. The clients, concerned owners who value their animals and consider them part of the family, want to be sure that everything medically possible is being done for their pets.

Dr. Theresa Ortega is one of three specialists in internal medicine working at the clinic. There are also two soft tissue surgeons and an orthopedic surgeon. These veterinarians have gone beyond their basic degrees as doctors of veterinary medicine to specialize, just as physicians who treat humans specialize.

"It is a very stressful job," Theresa says. "We're a twenty-four-hour practice, and you see a lot of animals that are on the brink of death because they have very serious problems. That's stressful. I'm pulled in a million directions all the time—a vet calling about a case I saw three years ago, or an owner calling, or there's a crisis happening in the back, or there's somebody up in the front room. I have to be very flexible and just go with the flow."

Because the animals are very sick, they may come in at any time of the night, and the staff will need to be there to get them started on treatment, or at least diagnosed. "There's a huge time commitment," Theresa says. "I think internal medicine is probably the worst that way. I don't have a nine-to-five job and I never will."

When asked when she knew she wanted to become a veterinarian, Theresa Ortega gets a puzzled look on her face. It's as though she were asked when she knew she wanted to breathe. It seems there was never a time when she didn't want to be a veterinarian.

Theresa was born in Mission Hills, California, on March 28, 1966. Her grandparents on her father's side were immigrants from Michoacán and Jalisco in Mexico. Her mother's great-grandparents were from Europe. Theresa's parents were born in the United States and met at San José State College, where Theresa's father was studying engineering. Then they moved to Los Angeles, where her father got his master's in acoustical engineering at UCLA.

Theresa has four older brothers. The oldest one is a biology professor in a college in Colorado; the second is a sports writer for the *Los Angeles Times*; the third has a management position in a water company; and the fourth is an electrical engineer. "My parents didn't push education," Theresa remembers, "it was just understood that if we wanted to, we could be whatever we wanted to be. They never made us come home and do our homework or whatever. My oldest brother had a big influence on me because he was always motivated to do well and go to college. I know a lot of people push their children very hard, but my parents weren't like that."

The public school Theresa attended in the San Fernando Valley area tested her when she was in first grade, and as a result she was put in honors classes. The school system had a magnet program that allowed students to go to the schools they chose. "From junior high on there was a group of about twenty of us who were always in the same classes," Theresa says. "The kids that I grew up with were academically motivated. I think I got a good education and preparation for college. That wasn't an obstacle for me the way it can be for some people, depending on where they grow up."

The biggest obstacle Theresa encountered was financial. Her parents couldn't afford to pay for her college education. After she graduated from Kennedy High School in Granada Hills, she was in a summer program at the University of California at Davis. She thought that she would go back home afterward and commute to Cal State Northridge. But she had also applied to Davis and got a scholarship to go there, so when the summer was over, she stayed.

The scholarship wasn't enough to live on, so she worked 20 to 30 hours a week while she was in college. She always shared a room, and she didn't have a car for six years—she rode her bike. "There were lots of ways I could save on money to get by," she remembers, "and I did. But it was worth it, and I really enjoyed going to school there. I knew I wanted to be a vet. . . . I always said I wanted to be a veterinarian. I don't know how I knew."

While Theresa was growing up, her family had a German shepherd, and she was the one who took care of him. She and her best friend always took their dogs along when they did things. The Ortega family couldn't have cats because three of the boys were allergic to them, so Theresa would play with the cats at her friends' homes. "I can't explain it," she says. "I just thought that if any animal was suffering, I'd want to help it."

While she was an undergraduate at Davis, she did explore other options, just in case she couldn't get into the veterinary program. She considered nutrition and physical fitness, which were, and still are, strong interests of hers. But she knew that if she could do it, she wanted to be a vet, and she did everything she could to improve her chances.

During her undergraduate years at Davis, Theresa would go back to Southern California in the summer and work, usually in veterinary clinics. That way she got the practical experience that made her even more certain about her decision to be a vet. Theresa recommends that anyone considering veterinary medicine should have this kind of practical experience: "I don't think veterinary medicine is for somebody who can't handle animals who are suffering or who are sick. Because sometimes they have to suffer before they can get better. That's something that weeds a lot of people out—besides grades. Another big thing is when they start doing the work. They say, 'Oh my god, I can't tolerate this. I can't stand seeing an animal that is sick.'"

Theresa's work experience in veterinary clinics also made her aware of how good the school at Davis was. After she graduated with her bachelor of science in biology in 1988, she was accepted into the veterinary medicine program at Davis.

She worked in the AIDS lab that developed tests for the disease. At that time UC Davis was doing all the testing for AIDS in California. It was also the campus where the virus for feline AIDS was discovered. "Basically while I was there I was getting experience in all sorts of areas," Theresa says. "That's why I wanted to go there. I was pretty determined that I was going to do it."

While she was in the veterinary medicine program at UC Davis, Theresa Ortega was also involved in a program for ethnic minority students and students from backgrounds that put them at a disadvantage. The program aimed to improve their application skills, teach the kind of experience they needed, and help them go through the interview process. She worked with these students the entire time she was there. They would spend half a day in classes and half a day at the veterinary teaching hospital, rotating just like the regular students did. They also had preparation classes for the Graduate Records Exam, the test they would have to take to get into graduate school.

"It was a very intense program," Theresa remembers. "They were doing something from eight in the morning until eight or nine at night. It was mostly people who were at Davis, because they had the information about it. But it was a good program, and I really enjoyed it."

The last two years that Theresa was there, they also had a summer program for disadvantaged high school students who had an interest in science. Those students didn't live on campus, but they'd come in every day, rotate in labs and the veterinary hospital, and get exposed to what veterinary school was all about. During these two years,

Theresa was also on the admissions committee for the program.

The aim of the program was to increase the diversity of the school and provide greater opportunity for students who were of ethnic minority groups or who had a disadvantaged background or both. Various factors were considered in evaluating the applicants: Grade point average was part of it, but letters of recommendation and experience were also considered.

"So that was my part," Theresa says, "evaluating these people. Were they going to be able to handle that school? Should we really push for them? . . . I thought it was a good program. We had people who came through and did a good job. One of the women who came through, she became a resident just like I was two years later. And she did a great job. There was no way she would have gotten into vet school otherwise because her grades while she was in early college would have pulled her down. She had this background that didn't prepare her right. But she did fantastic work."

After Dr. Ortega became a doctor of veterinary medicine, or D.V.M., in 1992, she went on to do an internship in small animal medicine and surgery at Santa Cruz Veterinary Hospital in Santa Cruz, California. She then returned to UC Davis to do her residency in the teaching hospital. Her specialty is in small animal internal medicine. After finishing her advanced work, she became an associate instructor at UC Davis for one year, teaching junior veterinary students. In addition, she has published much research and has received numerous awards for her research and clinical work.

The teaching of veterinary medicine has changed a little in recent years. Although the physiology of different animals is basically the same, the medical faculties have realized that there is so much to know that the students are allowed to do different tracking. "When I was there," Theresa remembers, "you couldn't track until your senior year. That meant you had to take all the horse classes, all the cow classes, all the small animal classes. Then they changed that. They found that people were coming out very broad based, but they weren't equipped to start a small animal medicine job, or an equine job, because they didn't have enough time to learn enough about that field. They were just getting a smattering. So they changed it so now you can choose where you want to go from your first year."

When she moved back to Southern California, Dr. Ortega worked for a while for VCA, a huge corporation that owns animal hospitals throughout the United States. Although she liked the people, she felt that her specialized training was being wasted in a general practice. When an opportunity to work with the Veterinary Medical and Surgical Group in Ventura came up in 1997, she took it.

"This position has worked out very well," Theresa says. "Before, because I had spent four extra years training, I felt like I was wasting it. And here I started an internship program. We have five interns who come here every year. We rank them, and they rank us, and the computer matches us up." The interns come from all over the United States and even from Canada.

Theresa Ortega's advice for any young person interested in a career as a veterinarian is to keep working on getting good grades. "Don't slack off, make that a priority. And then, get experience in the field and make sure that's what you want to do."

Dr. Eloy Rodriguez

Toxicologist, Cornell University

Eloy Rodriguez was born on January 7, 1947, in Edinburg, Texas, a little town near the coast in the southern tip of the state. In an article in *The New York Times Magazine* (one of many articles about Dr. Rodriguez's life and work), he is quoted as saying, "We were so poor that crime really didn't pay. It really didn't. I mean, who do you steal from in a neighborhood like ours?"

There is no question that the neighborhood was poor—its county is the poorest per capita in the entire United States. It was poor, but it was full of family. Besides Eloy's parents— his mother, who was from a family that had lived in Texas for generations; his father, who had come from Mexico as a bracero; and Eloy's younger brother and two sisters—there were aunts and uncles and cousins all living within a five-block area.

Eloy's family was remarkable. Although his parents and aunts and uncles were not educated people and were making a bare living with their hands and backs, they had a deep respect for education and an understanding of its importance. Of 67 Rodriguez cousins, 64 graduated from college and 11 earned advanced degrees. Although the adults were not educated—Eloy's father hadn't gone beyond first grade and his mother left school in the seventh grade—they were bilingual and had strong self-esteem. Eloy's mother made sure he went to school every day, and she went to PTA meetings to be sure her children were treated fairly.

Some of Eloy's earliest memories include the visits he made to his grandfather's farm in Mexico. "He would always take me out and show me animals and plants," Eloy remembers. "I was intrigued with them, and I think it just stayed with me." He also remembers being sick and taking medicinal herbs from an aunt's garden. When he got a little older, he worked in the fields as a migrant farmworker with his family, picking cotton and strawberries. He hated the work, but he was always interested in observing nature and growing things.

In the autobiography that Eloy Rodriguez wrote for the Society for the Advancement of Chicanos and Native Americans in Science (SACNAS), he records some of the observations he made as he was growing up: "Non-minorities ran the schools, the places of work, the government, and every other institution. . . . The students at my school were almost all Chicano, but hardly any of the kids in the accelerated learning classes were Chicanos. I knew that something was not right about this situation."

The public schools in Texas in the 1950s actively discouraged children from speaking Spanish, devising various punishments such as hitting their hands and having them write "I will not speak Spanish" on the board. Eloy's high school counselor tried to sign him up for vocational school for mechanics even though he hated fixing machinery. In spite of the negative attitudes he faced from his teachers, Eloy had a perfect attendance record from elementary school through high school and was an excellent student. He liked chemistry, art, and English particularly. Instead of listening to his counselor, Eloy enrolled at the University of Texas at Edinburg (now University of Texas–Pan American).

His original aim in college was to become an accountant. In an article about him in *Current Biography,* he is quoted as saying, "As an undergraduate I felt very lonely. I was one of a very

small number of minority students. There were no programs for minority students. We were kind of abandoned. It was like shopping at a 7-Eleven store, you know—just get your stuff and get out."

Despite the lack of any encouragement—he says he saw his first snowflake before he saw his first Hispanic scientist—Eloy was drawn to the sciences. When he transferred to the University of Texas at Austin, he changed his major to zoology and also studied botany and organic chemistry. As part of a work-study program, he got a job as a janitor in a research lab where one of the postdoctoral researchers showed him how to do chemical separations to isolate specific substances. The professor in charge of the lab, Dr. Tom J. Mabry, became Eloy's mentor. By the time he received his degree in zoology in 1969, Eloy Rodriguez was helping to manage the lab.

"I was really good at it," Dr. Rodriguez remembers. "The research bug got to me, the passion, the excitement of science. Once it gets you, you can't let go of it." He earned his Ph.D. in phytochemistry and plant biology from the University of Texas in 1975 and accepted a postdoctoral fellowship at the University of British Columbia in Vancouver, Canada, in 1975–76.

In 1976 he accepted the position of assistant professor in the Phytochemical Laboratory at the University of California at Irvine. "All along," he told an interviewer, "I was very aware that I was the first this, the first that, and I knew, I *knew* these guys were waiting for me to slip up." His response was to work 18 hours a day, practically living in the lab while he wrote scientific paper after scientific paper to satisfy the "publish or perish" pressure of the academic world. In 1983 he also began working as a professor in the Environmental Toxicology Program at UC Irvine.

Even though he then had two jobs instead of one, he got married and reduced his working day to only 14 hours. Eloy and his wife, Latina fiction writer Helena Viramontes, have two children, Pilar and Francisco. Having children of his own made Eloy Rodriguez aware that not much had changed since he had earned his doctorate. Latino scientists were still a rarity. He became a role model to school children, bringing them to his lab and setting up science programs for minority students called KIDS (Kids Investigating and Discovering Science). Dr. Rodriguez's program helped to more than double the number of Latino students majoring in the sciences at Irvine.

But as important as he thought it was to let minority students know how exciting careers in science can be—and he still thinks so and devotes a lot of time and energy to these efforts—his first love is science.

Many of Dr. Eloy Rodriguez's early ideas and scientific papers were about the chemical compounds in a plant of the Compositae family, which he found growing in a vacant lot near his college apartment in Texas. This plant family has many members, including sunflowers, daisies, and asters. He heard that there was a similar plant that grew in Mexico and received a grant to go find it. "Every plant chemist has his family," Dr. Rodriguez says, "and the Compositae is mine."

Because Dr. Rodriguez was an expert in the chemical properties of plants in the Compositae family, in 1984 Harvard University primatologist Richard Wrangham called on him for help on a project. Dr. Wrangham was observing the feeding habits of apes and monkeys in the forests of Uganda. He saw sick chimpanzees swallowing the bitter leaves of Aspilia plants. The plants tasted so awful the chimps were making faces, but they were eating them anyway. Dr. Wrangham wondered why.

Since Aspilia plants are part of the Compositae family, Dr. Rodriguez went to Uganda to observe the chimps himself. He took leaves from the Aspilia plants back to his laboratory and analyzed them. He found that they contained thiarubrine, a chemical that is toxic to some fungi and viruses. He proposed that the chimpanzees were using the leaves as medicine to kill the intestinal parasites that were plaguing them.

In 1989 Dr. Rodriguez and Dr. Wrangham announced a new field of study, which they called zoopharmacognosy. This means "animal knowledge of medicine." Since then Rodriguez and Wrangham have watched sick mountain gorillas in the wild also seeming to use plants to heal themselves. In 1992 the scientists presented their findings at a meeting of the American Association for the Advancement of Science. Other animal scientists began to report their own observations of animals seeming to use natural medicines.

Some other scientists didn't agree that the animals were making conscious decisions to eat particular plants for medical reasons. "Of course these questions should be asked," Dr. Rodriguez admitted, adding that he asks them himself. "But that doesn't mean you don't explore this [newfound] behavior. Why are the chimpanzees going after plants that are really bitter, that taste foul to them? Why do they choose that plant, that leaf, and how do they learn to select them? It's a whole new field."

But whatever the animals think they're doing, or whether they think about it at all, Dr. Rodriguez's research has resulted in a number of important discoveries. His work with the Aspilia plant produced a potent antibiotic called thiarubrine-A. Others of his investigations have explored desert plants possibly useful as an energy source, natives of the Amazon using psychoactive drugs to cure themselves of parasitic worms, natural insecticides, and the biochemistry of chilis.

In 1994 Dr. Rodriguez became professor of environmental studies at Cornell University in Ithaca, New York. He works with both undergraduate and graduate students, providing them with topics for their research, taking them with him on field trips to the jungles of Africa and South America, to the islands of the Caribbean, or to any place from which reports reach him about curious plants and the animals that use them.

"When I do chemistry," he explained in a recent article, "I don't just do it for the sake of chemistry. It's exciting to look at new chemical structures, but I have always wanted to understand the reason for their existence. To do that you have to get out in the field. You have to learn to observe the natural world."

In a recent issue of the journal *Chemical Ecology,* some postdoctoral researchers at Cornell reported on the use of natural insecticides by capuchin monkeys. The monkeys catch millipedes and rub secretions from them onto their fur. This behavior occurs when the mosquitoes are most pesky. The researchers were able to demonstrate that the millipede secretions consist of only two chemicals, both in the benzoquinone family and both known to be powerful insect repellents. This instance of animals using chemicals medicinally would seem to be a persuasive example that confirms Dr. Rodriguez's theories.

Dr. Rodriguez has had over 150 articles published and has received over $12 million in research grants from various institutions. Because he is bilingual, he is able to speak with scientists in Mexico (where he received the Martin De La Cruz Silver Medal for Medicinal Research), Central and South America, and the Caribbean.

In a feature article about Dr. Eloy Rodriguez in the *Los Angeles Times* in March 2001, he offers some advice to young people considering careers in science:

1. Take a maverick approach to learning. Mavericks don't have to be told what to do. They go outside the norm to achieve what's important to them.

2. Prepare yourself for your profession. Read outside the classroom.

3. Become strongly disciplined. Your focus should be: I want to be the best at what I'm doing.

4. Try to connect things, for example, evolution, biology, anthropology. . . learn to build bridges between the courses you take.

5. Find good mentors who are in many ways like you. Everyone who has been successful in life has had a teacher or mentor to help him or her.

Dr. Richard Tapia

Professor of Computational Applied Mathematics at Rice University

Dr. Richard Tapia enjoys being a mathematics professor. The two major aspects of his job, research and teaching, are equally important to him. He finds that explaining math to students helps him understand his own work better, and his own work clarifies his explanations to students. "The issue of publishing new mathematics is critical," he says. "You have to publish, you have to succeed in your research at a research university. . . It's been the focal point of my success. I do good teaching, I've won awards, and they complement each other."

In addition to his teaching and research, Dr. Tapia is involved in outreach education, which means that he lectures, gives interviews on radio and television, and appears as a speaker when asked to do so—all for the purpose of letting young Latinos and their parents know that education is the key to a successful career. He is on the National Science Board and the governing board of the National Science Foundation, and he is a member of the National Academy of Engineering, so he frequently travels to Washington, D.C. "I don't know how to say no," he says. "I end up doing too many things, being a member of too many committees, traveling too much. 'Too much' doesn't mean that I don't enjoy it, but that I neglect parts of my family life or other things. The only drawback of my career is that it has allowed me to do too many wonderful things."

To Richard Tapia, mathematics is beautiful, exciting, and fulfilling. He is able to use mathematics in many areas of his life. In addition to his position at Rice University, he is an adjunct faculty member of Baylor School of Medicine. He uses mathematics with the computer to try to find optimal treatment—how much medicine to use and when—for the autoimmune disease that has confined his wife to a wheelchair: multiple sclerosis. Many of the problems on which he works come from the area of biology. For example, he uses mathematics to learn more about proteins and viruses.

Dr. Tapia has always loved cars and racing, and his son enjoys bicycle racing. He finds that mathematics helps him understand many subtle aspects of racing. One lecture he gives to young students shows them how math helps him to understand the mechanics of racing.

"Mathematics is a separate study and discipline," Dr. Tapia says, "but it's also a language that describes the world we live in. And particularly the world of science. Once you describe the world, then you can play with it. What if I change this? What if I do that? To me mathematics is wonderful. And I'm not a one-dimensional nerd. I don't just stay in mathematics and can't talk about anything else. I can talk about many topics. . . . I feel mathematics is a wonderful background."

Dr. Tapia's success, as he is quick to tell, comes from his parents' guidance and strength. His mother, Magdalena Angulo, was born in the mountains of Chihuahua, Mexico. When she was 11 years old, she and her 10-year-old sister came to the United States by themselves. Magda was sent by their father in search of education. She stayed with a distant relative in Los Angeles for a while, but when she finished middle school, the man told her, "Girls don't need an education. You have to go to work." He said she couldn't go to high school, so she moved out. She put her younger sister in a church home while she lived with a Jewish family, cooking and cleaning for them while she went to high school.

Amado Tapia, Richard's father, was born in Nayarit, Mexico, and came to the United States with two older brothers when he was about eight or nine. They also lived in Los Angeles; they worked in landscaping. Eventually Amado and Magdalena met each other, married, and started their own landscaping business. Of Magda and Amado Tapia's five children, two have graduate degrees and two others are lawyers.

"My mother was very, very strong on teaching us that we were as good as anyone, that no one was better than anyone else," Richard Tapia remembers. "My mother really believed that all people were created equal. In that, she allowed me to use peer evaluation—I would say, 'Okay, you're doing that, therefore I can do it. If you're going to college, then I can go to college. If you're going to grad school, then I can go to grad school. If you can be a Ph.D., then I can be a Ph.D.' My mother instilled in us the feeling that we were every bit as good as anybody. Whenever we did something it was a global issue—not 'That's pretty good for your family,' or 'That's pretty good for someone from our neighborhood.' It was either good or bad across the board."

Richard and his twin brother were born in 1939 in Santa Monica. Richard was always extremely good at math. In first, second, and third grade, he was the best in his class. He says that it wasn't a case of having seven talents and choosing one. It was always clear that mathematics was his field. By fifth grade his teacher said, "You already know this math, so you help the other kids." It wasn't that he had seen the material before—he just knew it immediately. All the way through high school and for the first two years of college he was always at the top of his class in math. Not until he transferred to the University of California at Los Angeles did he meet people who were as skilled as he was.

The schools attended by Richard and his brothers and sisters weren't the best. They were in poor parts of town, didn't have the best teachers, and most of the students didn't care about education. It wasn't until he was in community college that Richard found teachers who took an interest in him and told him he should go to UCLA. "I didn't have a plan," he says, "I just bounced off the walls. But there were people along the way who helped me

when I got lost or misguided. Here's what my mother taught me: Go forward. Take one step at a time, take two, take three, and eventually you're going to end up in a situation that is rewarding. But I didn't know where the end of the path was at all."

Even though he didn't receive a lot of encouragement in school—in fact, sometimes his teachers didn't seem to like him—Richard always liked himself. "We're all real confident," he says. "My brothers and sisters are that way, too. As I grew up, I liked who I was. I liked the person that I was. I liked my background. I loved growing up Mexican American. People told me that I would have to change. I've never changed. I learned how to be bicultural, how to succeed in a world that was different from the culture I had grown up in. I also learned how not to give up the culture that I grew up with. So I'm happy that I haven't changed. I'm still the person that I liked many years ago."

In addition to mathematical talent, the main qualification that Richard Tapia had for his career, and the one he says is necessary for anyone going into the field of math and science, is the love of it. After that you need preparation. He teaches his students that they don't have to work 24 hours a day. They should mix work with play the way he did.

Dr. Tapia's path led to a bachelor of science degree from UCLA in 1961. From there he went to Todd Shipyards in San Pedro, California, where he worked on a research project for two years. He then returned to UCLA to work on his Ph.D. After earning the doctorate in 1968, he worked at the University of Wisconsin as an assistant professor for two years. In 1970 he was recruited by Rice University in Houston, Texas. With the exception of 1976, which he spent at Stanford University, Dr. Tapia has been at Rice ever since.

When asked how accessible the field of mathematics is for Latinos, Dr. Tapia said that someone who has a degree in computer science or mathematics will be able to get a very good job with a good salary. "There is so much need for people with mathematical understanding," he says. "For example, the schools are in crisis mode right now—one of the serious deficiencies of our public school system is that we don't have enough people educated in mathematics who want to teach. . . . There are jobs at all levels, and if you're willing to say, 'This is the job that I'll

be most effective at,' there are going to be jobs."

According to Dr. Tapia, there are also many opportunities for people with a math background to go into the business world. In finance, for example, Wall Street is hiring many people. The information technology workforce is looking for people educated in math and computer science. People with bachelor's degrees are hired at as much as $100,000 per year. And then, of course, there are the positions in education. With Ph.D.'s it depends on the situation; starting salaries might be around $50,000 but could eventually go up as high as $200,000. "I've never produced a Ph.D. student who couldn't get a choice of jobs," Dr. Tapia says. "As long as you are open to the options that are available, you're going to be fine. If you nail yourself and say, 'The only position I'll accept is one at Harvard,' then of course that probably won't happen."

When asked if there were other Latino mathematicians who inspired him, Dr. Tapia said, "At UCLA Dr. David Sanchez, a fellow Mexican American, served as mentor and role model. There are very few Latino mathematicians produced in this country; however, there are a few very good ones. There are Latinos who come from other countries and become university professors, but for Latinos raised in the United States, the number is very small, almost nonexistent, in math, computer science, and the physical sciences. We don't have representation, we don't have role models, we don't have the individuals in decision-making positions. In 1992, I was the first native-born Latino elected to the National Academy of Engineering. The academy is a very prestigious group of people who have succeeded in some aspect of computer science or engineering. To wait until 1992 was too late; with our talents as a group, we should have been there long before."

Dr. Tapia was appointed by President Bill Clinton to the National Science Board. He is the only U.S.-born Hispanic on the board. He makes the point that there aren't enough Latinos to take the leadership positions in education, science, and engineering that are available in this country, and that Latinos must take these positions if the situation is to improve.

The advice Richard Tapia has for young Latinos just setting out on their own career paths is basically the attitude that sustained his mother, 11-year-old Magdalena, when she set out with her younger sister to make her way to a strange country three-quarters of a century ago:

"Don't sell yourself short. Believe that you can do what you want to do and then go for it. There are many paths to the same place. Don't stop when you could have gone further. Just believe that you can." Magdalena Tapia went to college herself after her husband died when she was 65. She earned her translator's certificate and for several years worked as a translator for medical and legal offices in Los Angeles, where there were clients who did not speak English.

Richard Tapia remembers that because he was a first-generation Mexican American born in a very poor part of Los Angeles, nobody thought he would make it to many of the places he has. "But the belief in myself and the values that my mother taught me took me there," he says. "Years ago, my mother used to tell me these things and I used to say, 'Mom, you're wrong!' But I've learned that she was right. So the thing that I have to say now is, 'Just believe that you can.' You have to be dedicated, and you have to be willing to not give up."

PART
3

Resources

Books and Directories 88

Internet Sources 90

Master Index to Careers 92

Master Index to People Profiled 94

Index to this book 96

Books and Directories

Careers in Health Care

Bai, Xinghua, and R. B. Baron. *Acupuncture in Clinical Practice: A Practical Guide to the Use of Acupuncture and Related Therapies.* Newton, MA: Butterworth-Heinemann, 1996.

Camenson, Blythe. *Real People Working in Health Care.* Lincolnwood, IL: NTC Publishing Group, 1997.

Cargill, Marie. *Acupuncture: A Viable Medical Alternative.* Westport, CT: Praeger Publishers, 1994.

Chiropractic Business Management Guide. Needham Heights, MA: Ginn Press, 1999.

Chiropractors. Moravia, NY: Chronicle Guidance Publications, Inc., 1995.

Clayton, Lawrence. *Careers in Psychology,* revised edition. New York: Rosen Group, 1996.

Coles, Robert. *Mind's Eye: A Psychiatrist Looks at His Profession.* Boston: Little, Brown, 1996.

Cook, Trevor. *Homeopathic Medicine Today: A Study.* New Canaan, CT: Keats Publishing, 1989.

Coon, Dennis. *Essentials of Psychology,* 7th edition. St. Paul, MN: West Publishing Co., 1996.

Damp, Dennis V. *Health Care Job Explosion.* Moon Township, PA: Bookhaven Press, 1998.

Fox, Arnold, and Barry Fox. *Alternative Healing: Nontraditional Therapies Such as Acupuncture, Homeopathy, and Nutritional Healing Can Help You Cope with Illnesses from Allergies to Ulcers.* Franklin Lakes, NJ: Career Press, Inc., 1996.

Garrett, Raymond J., and Teressa Stone. *Catching Good Health with Homeopathic Medicine: A Concise Self-Help Introduction to Homeopathy.* Sebastopol, CA: CRCS Publications, 1991.

Hammon, Christopher. *Complete Family Guide to Homeopathy: An Encyclopedia of Safe and Effective Remedies.* New York: Viking Penguin Press, 1996.

Job Opportunities in Health Care. Princeton, NJ: Peterson's Guides, 1995.

Keyes, Fenton. *Opportunities in Psychiatry.* Lincolnwood, IL: VGM Career Horizons, 1994.

Klitzman, Robert. *In a House of Dreams and Glass: Becoming a Psychiatrist.* New York: Ivy Books, 1996.

Lazarus, Arthur, ed. *Career Pathways in Psychiatry: Transition in Changing Times.* Hillsdale, NJ: Analytic Press, 1996.

Palmer, D. D. *The Chiropractor.* Kilo, MT: Kessinger Publishing Co., 1996.

Perry, Philip A. *Opportunities in Mental Health Careers.* Lincolnwood, IL: VGM Career Horizons, 1996.

Peterson, Dennis, and Glenda Wiese. *Chiropractic: An Illustrated History.* St. Louis, MO: Mosby-Year Book, Inc., 1994.

Pirog, John E. *The Practical Application of Meridian Style Acupuncture.* Berkeley, CA: Pacific View Press, 1996.

Sacks, Terence. *Careers in Medicine.* Lincolnwood, IL: VGM Career Books, 1997.

Schafer, R. C., and Louis Spartelli. *Opportunities in Chiropractic Careers.* Lincolnwood, IL: NTC/Contemporary Publishing Co., 1997.

Selden, Arnette. *VGM's Handbook of Health Care Careers.* Lincolnwood, IL: NTC/Contemporary Publishing Co., 1993.

Simpson, Carolyn, and Penelope Hall. *Careers in Medicine.* New York: Rosen Publishing Group, 1994.

Steinfeld, Alan. *Careers in Alternative Health Care.* New York: Rosen Group, 1996

Sternberg, Robert J. *Career Paths in Psychology: Where Your Degree Can Take You.* Washington, DC: American Psychological Association, 1997.

Ullman, Dana. *Discovering Homeopathy: Your Introduction to the Science and Art of Homeopathic Medicine.* Berkeley, CA: North Atlantic Books, 1991.

Careers in Science

Camenson, Blythe. *Careers for Plant Lovers and Other Green Thumb Types.* Lincolnwood, IL: VGM Career Horizons, NTC Publishing Group, 1995.

The Complete Guide to Environmental Careers in the 21st Century. Washington, DC: Island Press, 1999.

Dixon, Dougal, ed. *The Practical Geologist.* New York: Simon and Schuster Trade, 1992.

Goldsmith, Donald, ed. *The Astronomers.* New York: St. Martin's Press, 1993.

Heitzmann, William R. *Opportunities in Marine and Maritime Careers.* Lincolnwood, IL: NTC/Contemporary Publishing Co., 1994.

Kuton, William T., ed. *Biological Science.* New York: W.W. Norton & Co., Inc., 1996.

Leonick, Michael, ed. *The Light at the Edge of the Universe: Astronomers on the Front Lines of the Cosmological Revolution.* New York: Random House, Inc., 1993.

Louise, Chandra B. *Jump Start Your Career in Bio Science.* Durham, NC: Peer Productions, 1998.

Miller, Louise. *Careers for Nature Lovers and Other Outdoor Types.* Lincolnwood, IL: VGM Career Horizons, NTC Publishing Group, 1992.

Physical Sciences, Mathematics, Agricultural Sciences. Princeton, NJ: Peterson's, 1998.

Quintana, Debra. *100 Jobs in the Environment.* New York: Simon and Schuster Macmillan Co., 1996.

Salaries of Scientists, Engineers, and Technicians: A Summary of Salary Surveys. Washington, DC: Commission on Professionals in Science and Technology, 1993.

White, William C. *Opportunities in Farming and Agricultural Careers.* Lincolnwood, IL: VGM Career Horizons, NTC Publishing Group, 1995.

Willie, Christopher M. *Opportunities in Forestry Careers.* Lincolnwood, IL: NTC/Contemporary Publishing Co., 1998.

Wood, Richard A. *Weather Almanac.* Farmington Hills, MI: The Gale Group, 1997.

Woodburn, John H. *Opportunities in Chemistry Careers.* Lincolnwood, IL: NTC/Contemporary Publishing Co., 1997.

Internet Sources

General Career Information

Peterson's: www.petersons.com

Scientific Staffing: www.scientificstaffing.com

U.S. Government Office of Personnel Management: www.usajobs.opm.gov

Health Care Organizations

Accrediting Bureau of Health Education Schools: www.abhes.org

Acupuncture: www.acupuncture.com

Allied Health Personnel in Ophthalmology: www.jcahpo.org

American Association of Colleges of Osteopathic Medicine: www.aacom.org

American Association of Colleges of Pharmacy: www.aacp.org

American Association of Colleges of Podiatric Medicine: www.aacpm.org

American Association of Dental Schools: www.aads.jhu.edu

American Association of Medical Assistants: www.aama-ntl.org

American Association of Oriental Medicine: www.aaom.org

American Association for Respiratory Care: www.aarc.org

American Chiropractic Association: www.amerchiro.org

American Dental Association: www.ada.org

American Health Information Management Association: www.ahima.org

American Medical Association: www.ama-assn.org

American Medical Technologists: www.amtl.com

American Optometric Association: www.aoanet.org

American Osteopathic Association: www.aoa-net.org

American Pharmaceutical Association: www.aphanet.org

American Physical Therapy Association: www.apta.org

American Podiatric Medical Association: www.apma.org

American Psychiatric Association: www.psych.org

American Society of Clinical Pathologists: www.ascp.org

American Society of Consultant Pharmacists: www.ascp.com

American Society of Health-System Pharmacists: www.ashp.org

Association of American Medical Colleges: www.aamc.org

Association of Schools and Colleges of Optometry: www.opted.org

Committee on Accreditation for Respiratory Care: www.coarc.com

Dental Assisting National Board, Inc.: www.dentalassisting.com

Dynamic Chiropractic: www.chiroweb.com

Federation of Chiropractic Licensing Boards: www.fclb.org

International Chiropractic Association: www.chiropractic.org

National Acupuncture and Oriental Medicine Alliance: www.healthy.net/pan/pa/acupuncture/naoma/index.html

National Association of Emergency Medical Technicians: www.naemt.org

National Board for Respiratory Care: www.nbrc.org

National Community Pharmacists Association: www.ncpanet.org

National League for Nursing: www.nln.org

National Registry of Emergency Medical Technicians: www.nremt.org

The Natural Pharmacist: www.tnp.com

Registered Medical Assistants of American Medical Technologists: www.amtl.com

Scientific Organizations

Accreditation Board for Engineering and Technology, Inc.: www.abet.org

Aerospace Industries Association: www.aia-aerospace.org

American Association of Petroleum Geologists: www.aapg.org

American Association of Pharmaceutical Scientists: www.aaps.org/sciaffairs/careerinps.htm

American Astronomical Society: www.aas.org

American Chemical Society: www.acs.org

American Geological Institute: www.agiweb.org

American Geophysical Union: www.agu.org

American Institute of Aeronautics and Astronautics: www.aiaa.org

American Institute of Biological Sciences: www.aibs.org

American Institute of Chemical Engineers: www.aiche.org

American Institute of Physics: www.aip.org

American Meteorological Society: www.ametsoc.org/AMS

American Nuclear Society: www.ans.org

American Physical Society: www.aps.org

American Society for Biochemistry and Molecular Biology: www.faseb.org/asbmb

American Society of Civil Engineers: www.asce.org

American Society for Microbiology: www.asmusa.org

Astronomer's Net: www.astonomers.net

Biotechnology Industry Organization: www.bio.org

Botanical Society of America: www.botany.org/bsa/careers

Careers in Astronomy: www.aas.org/~education/career.html

Geological Society of America: www.geosociety.org

Institute of Electrical and Electronics Engineers: www.ieee.org

Institute of Industrial Engineers, Inc.: www.iienet.org

Junior Engineering Technical Society: www.jets.org

Marine Technology Society: www.mtsociety.org

Minerals, Metals, and Materials Society: www.tms.org

National Aeronautical and Space Administration, NASA: www.nasa.gov

National Society of Professional Engineers: www.nspe.org

Smithsonian's Sources for Information on Careers in Biology, Conservation, and Oceanography: www.si.edu/resource/faq/nmnh/careers.htm

Society of American Foresters: www.safnet.org

Society of Exploration Geophysicists: www.seg.org

Master Index to Careers

actor/actress, En

acupuncturist, SM

administrative assistant, CS, Ed

advertising copywriter, En

advertising salesperson, PC

agent, En, Sp, MI

agriculturalist, SM

alternative medical practitioner, SM

ambassador, LP

animator, En

archaeologist, SM

arranger/orchestrator, MI

art director, PC

associate director, nonprofit organization, CS

astronomer, SM

athlete, professional, Sp

athletic director, Sp

athletic trainer, Sp

attorney *see* lawyer

bailiff, LP

baseball umpire, Sp

biologist, SM

board member, CS

broadcast engineer, PC

broadcaster *see also* journalist, CS

bus driver, Ed

business owner, LE

casting director, En

chemist, SM

chief executive officer/executive director/president, CS, LE

chiropractor, SM

choreographer, En

cinematographer (director of photography), En

city administrator, LP

classified worker, Ed

coach/manager, Ed, Sp

columnist, PC

comedian, En

comedy writer, En

communications/media relations/public relations officer, CS

community affairs director (television), En

composer, En

computer engineer, Tc

computer programmer, Tc

computer technician, Tc

control room engineer, MI

copyeditor, PC

copyist, MI

copywriter, PC

costume designer (theater/television/film), En

court reporter, LP

crime prevention specialist, LP

criminal defense lawyer, LP

critic/reviewer, En, MI

data base manager, Tc

data entry clerk, Tc

data processing technician, Tc

dental hygienist, SM

dentist, SM

director (feature films or television), En

disc jockey/radio announcer, PC, MI

editor, PC

engineer, SM

engineering technician, SM

equipment manager, Sp

FBI agent, LP

film editor, En

fingerprint expert, LP

football referee, Sp

foreign service officer, LP

forester, SM

founder, CS, LE

fund-raiser for nonprofit organization, CS

general manager (station manager), PC

KEY—What Book?
CS—Community Service
Ed—Education
En—Entertainment
LE—Latino Entrepreneurs
LP—Law and Politics
MI—Music Industry
PC—Publishing and Communications
SM—Science and Medicine
Sp—Sports
Tc—Technology

geologist, SM
government relations officer, LP
grant writer, CS
graphic designer, PC, Tc
graphics programmer, Tc
guidance counselor, Ed
home health care worker, CS
human rights worker, LP
immigration and customs officer, LP
instructional assistant, Ed
journalist, CS, En, LP, PC, Sp
judge, LP
justice of the peace, LP
juvenile detention officer, LP
labor representative (organizer, regional director),
    CS
laboratory technician, SM
lawyer (attorney, paralegal), CS, En, LP, Sp
    legal secretary, LP
librarian, Ed
lighting designer (theater), En
makeup artist (theater/television/film), En
manufacturer's representative, Sp
marketing director, Sp
medical doctor, CS, SM
medical scientist, SM
meteorologist/weather forecaster, PC, SM
news director, PC
news writer (radio), PC
notary public, LP
nurse, CS, SM
nutritionist, SM
optometrist, SM
paramedic, emergency medical technician (EMT),
    SM
parole officer, LP
personal manager, MI
personal trainer, Sp
pharmacist, SM
photographer or camera operator, PC
physical therapist, SM
physician, SM
physicist, SM
playwright, En
podiatrist, SM
police officer, LP
political lobbyist, LP
political strategist, LP
politician, LP
press agent, En

principal, Ed
probation officer, LP
producer, En
professional scout, Sp
professor, college or university, Ed
program director, PC
promoter, music and events, MI
proofreader, PC
psychiatrist, SM
psychologist, Ed, SM
public relations director, En, PC, Sp
publicist, Sp
publicity director, PC
publisher, PC
radio producer, PC
representative (Congress), LP
sales representative (books), PC
scenic designer (theater), En
science technician, SM
screenwriter, En
senator, LP
set designer (theater/television/film/video), En
singer, MI
songwriter, MI
sound editor, En
sports reporter/sportscaster, PC, Sp
stage director, En
stage manager, En
superintendent (school), Ed
systems analyst, Tc
teacher, Ed
    technical support specialist, Tc
technical writer, PC
television news anchor, PC
tour publicist, En
tuner, musical instruments, MI
translator/interpreter, LP
treaty negotiator, LP
veterinarian, SM
victim advocate, LP
Web master, Tc
writer, book, PC
youth coordinator, CS

Master Index
to People Profiled

Acosta, Angela, Media Relations, Community Relations Director, CS

Acrivos, Juana Vivó, Professor of Chemistry, SM

Ahmed, Ada Diaz, founder and president of failed Latina Web site, Tc

Alonso, José Jr., Physicist, SM

Alvarado, Linda, Baseball Team Owner, Sp

Alvarez, Joe, Police Officer, Supervisor of Crime Stoppers, LP

Anaya, Rudolfo, Writer , PC

Ancira, Ernesto, Car Dealer, LE

Arellano, Jairo, Assistant Principal, Ed

Baca, Bettie, Senior Executive Service Candidate, LP

Baca, James, Mayor, LP

Barbosa, Pedro, Entomologist, SM

Barrientos, Gonzalo, State Senator, LP

Belli, Gioconda, Writer, PC

Benitez, John "Jellybean," disc jockey, recording artist, record producer, MI

Bezos, Jeff, founder and CEO of on-line store, Tc

Brown, Sarita, Educational Programs Administrator, Ed

Burr, Ramiro, music critic, MI

Cardona, Carlos, founder and senior vice president of Hispanic Web site, Tc

Carrera, Mario M., Senior Media Sales Executive, PC

Casillas, Ederlen, Codirector of nonprofit organization, CS

Centeno, Oscar, Business Owner, Trucking Company, LE

Chavez, Gabriel, Business Owner, Technology Company, LE

Cuellar, Henry, Secretary of State (Texas), LP

Davidds-Garrido, Norberto, professional football player, Sp

de la Hoya, Oscar, Professional Boxer, Sp

Del Olmo, Frank, Vice President of Professional Programs, CS

Del Toro, Benicio, Actor, En

Diaz, Freddy, graphic artist and graphic arts teacher, Tc

Diaz, Guadalupe "Aura," computer artist, Tc

Dominguez, Isabel, Geneticist, SM

Escalante, Jaime, Math Teacher, Ed, SM

Esparza, Moctesuma, Producer, En

Fernandez, Lisa, Softball Player, Sp

Flores, Tom, Football Coach, Sp

Galindo, Max, Paramedic, SM

Garcia, Abraham and Ana Corinna, Business Owners, Computer Company, LE

Garcia, Paul, Web master, Tc

Garcia, Rodolfo, Relationship Banker, LP

Gates, Ann Quiroz, computer science professor, Tc

Girón, Carlos, Sports Publicist, Sp

Gomez, Julio, founder and owner of e-commerce consulting firm, Tc

Gonzales, Enrique, project manager for a network of Web sites, Tc

Gonzales, Thomas, technology consultant, Tc

Gonzales, Victor, computer programmer, Tc

Gonzalez, Alex, Baseball Player, Sp

Gonzalez, Larry, Executive Director, LP

Guerrero, Lena, Political Lobbyist, LP

Gutiérrez, Margo, Librarian, Ed

Guzman-Macias, Estela, Special Education Teacher, Resource Specialist, Ed

Hayek, Salma Actress, En

Henley, Maria Jimenez, Stage Manager, Assistant Director, Choreographer, and Dancer, En

Hernandez, Antonia, Lawyer, President, CS

Hernandez, Fidel, Zoologist, SM

Hernandez, G. Herb, County Councilman at Large, LP

Hernandez-Castillo, Bel, Publisher, Editor-in-Chief, Dancer, and Actress, En

Herrera, Leticia, Business Owner, Cleaning Service, LE

Heumann, Judith, Assistant Secretary for Special Education, Ed

Jaime, Mental Health Technician, SM

Jimenez, James, City Administrator, LP

Kanellos, Nicolás, Book Publisher, PC

Leanos, John, Cultural Worker, Artist, LE

Leguizamo, John, Actor, Comedian, Playwright, En

Leoni, Dennis Edward, Writer, Producer, En

Llamosa, Carlos, Soccer Player, Sp
Llanos, Regla "Toni," dancer, choreographer, MI
Lopez, George, Comedian, En
Los Lobos (David Hidalgo, Conrad Lozano, Louie Perez, and Cesar Rosas), musicians, MI
Martin, Maria Emilia, Executive Producer, PC
Martinez, Christine, radio disc jockey, MI
Martinez, Gilbert, Chief Judge, LP
Martinez, Rueben, Bookstore Owner, PC
Martinez, Walter, Magazine Publisher, Editor, PC
Massó, Jose, Center for the Study of Sport in Society, Sp
McBride, Theresa, computer systems consultant, Tc
Melendez, Bill, Animator, Producer, En
Mendoza, Araceli, Business Owner, Beauty Salon, LE
Mendoza, Graciela Contreras, Head Start Teacher, Ed
Monterroso, Benjamin, Labor Leader, CS
Morales, Dionicio, Founder and President, CS
Morales, Hugo, Radio Station Executive Director, PC
Moran, Julio, Executive Director of nonprofit organization, CS
Moreno, Richard Blackburn, President of nonprofit organization, CS
Moreno, Rita, Actress, Performer, En
Muniz, Marc Anthony, singer, MI
Nava, Gregory, Director, Writer, En
Nuñez, Emanuel, Agent, En
Nuñez, Tommy, Referee, Sp
O'Brien, Soledad, Television News Anchor, PC
Oceguera, Frank, III, Math Teacher, Ed
Olmos, Edward James, Actor, En
Ortega, Juan C., Design Firm President, Creative Director, PC
Ortega, Theresa, Veterinarian, SM
Penelas, Alex, Executive Mayor, LP
Perez, Lisandro, Sociology Professor, Ed
Perez, Pamela, Latino News Reporter, LP
Perez, Severo, Writer, Director, Producer, En
Porras-Field, Esperanza, Business Owner, Consulting Firm, Real Estate, LE
Portillo, Wendy, process control analyst, Tc
Ramirez, Eddie, promoter and event organizer, MI
Ramirez,Eddie, Promoter, event organizer, MI
Ramos, Jorge, Television News Anchor, PC
Rivas, Yolanda, manager of on-line software products, Tc
Roa, Horacio, practitioner of holistic medicine, SM

Rodriguez, Douglas, Chef and Restaurant Owner, LE
Rodriguez, Eloy, Toxicologist, SM
Rodriguez, Rick, Newspaper Senior Vice President, Executive Editor, PC
Rojas, Nydia, singer, MI
Romo, Ricardo, University President, Ed
Ruiz, Hector de Jesus, president of microprocessor manufacturer, Tc
Ruiz, John, Boxer, Sp
Sanchez, Guillermo, Dentist, SM
Sanchez, Josephine, Associate Director, CS
Sanchez, Loretta, Congresswoman, LP
Santana, Carlos, musician, MI
Santiago, Esmeralda, Writer, PC
Soto, Hilda Lorenia, e-commerce consultant, Tc
Tapia, Richard, Professor of Computational Applied Mathematics, SM
Tinjaca, Mabel, Author and Consultant in Organizational Development, LE
Tobar, Hector, National News Correspondent, PC
Trujillo, Gary, CEO of a failed Internet company, Tc
Vargas, Garrett, Software Design Engineer, PC
Vargas, Juan, Business Owner, Pinatas, LE
Villa, Brenda, Water Polo Player, Sp
Villalobos, Reynaldo, Cinematographer, Director, En
Wilkins, Ron, Probation Supervisor, LP
Yzaguirre, Raul, Executive Director of nonprofit organization, CS, LP
Zamora, Guadalupe, Family Doctor, SM
Zamora, Jim, Crime Scene Detective, LP
Zamora, Maria, Paraprofessional Educator, Ed

Index

Acrivos, Juana Vivo - 39-41
acupuncture - 17, 22-23
agriculture - 9
   animals - 9, 63-64
   food - 9, 55
   plants - 9, 55, 75, 77
   soil - 9
Alonso, Jose - 42-49
Alcoholics Anonymous - 31
alternative medicine - 22-23
archeology - 9-10
astronomy - 10
Barbosa, Pedro - 8, 50-55
biology - 10-11, 70
   aquatic - 10-11
   ecology - 10, 54, 64
   entomology - 10, 51-55
   genetics - 57-61
   limnology - 10
   toxicology - 75-79
   zoology - 10, 63-67, 76
chemistry - 11, 39-43, 58
   analytical - 11
   organic - 11, 67, 75-79
   inorganic - 11, 37-41
   physical - 11, 41
   biochemistry - 11
Chinese medicine - 17, 22-23
chiropractic - 17, 19
dental hygienist - 19-20
dentistry - 20
Dominguez, Isabel - 56-61
EMT, emergency medical technician - 25-26, 29
engineering - 11-12,
   chemical - 12, 41
   civil - 12
   electrical - 12, 46
   industrial - 12
   mechanical - 12, 46, 61
   technician - 12
Escalante, Jaime - 8
family practice - 27
forestry - 13
geology - 13-14
   mineralogy - 13
   oceanography - 13

seismology - 13
herbology - 23
Hernandez, Fidel - 62-67
holistic medicine - 22-23
homeopathy - 23
laboratory technician - 20-21
licensed practical nurse - 21
massage therapy - 23
mathematics - 8, 10, 11, 16, 39, 46, 57, 81-85
medical science - 21, 57-61
mental health technician - 32
meteorology - 14
National Science Foundation - 40, 41
nurse practitioner - 22, 23
nursing - 21, 23-24
nursing aide - 24
nutrition - 22, 24-25
   clinical dietician - 24, 31
   community dietician - 25
optometry - 25
Ortega, Theresa - 78-73
paramedic -25-26, 29
pharmacist - 26
physician - 28, 30
physical therapy - 26, 28
physics - 14-15, 43-49
podiatry - 30
psychiatry - 30-31
psychology - 31
Roa, Horacio - 22-23
Rodriguez, Eloy - 74-79
Sanchez, Guillermo - 18-19
science technician - 15
Tapia, Richard - 80-85
shiatsu - 22
veterinarian - 31-33, 69-73
yoga - 22
Zamora, Guadalupe - 27